THE MIRROR OF LIFE AND DEATH

The author of this short book is a psychiatrist who has long studied the human mind from the viewpoint both of Depth Psychology and Theosophy. He combines with this the knowledge gained as a result of his wife's direct clairvoyant observation.

Dr. Bendit feels that, while birth is usually welcomed with joy, its complement — death — is wrongly feared and looked upon with horror. Yet death is as natural and inevitable as birth; and, moreover, it is felt to be so by the individual who has faced the issue clearly and prepared himself for it. Death is often a liberation, while birth may represent a limitation for the individual spirit. The author is not satisfied with over-simplified ideas about death, and makes a clear distinction between survival and immortality, and of those aspects of man which are involved.

Dr. Bendit also discusses a number of related problems such as communication with the dead, ghosts and haunts, and other more philosophical matters such as time and the relation between life in the sense of growth, and death as withdrawal or resolution.

This is a book which, while it carefully avoids dogmatizing, suggests explanations for some of the many problems which surround human life — and death.

THE MIRROR OF LIFE
AND DEATH

BY

LAURENCE J. BENDIT

A QUEST BOOK
Published under a grant from The Kern Foundation

THE THEOSOPHICAL PUBLISHING HOUSE
Wheaton, Ill., U.S.A.
Madras, India / London, England

DEDICATION

My wife, Phoebe Daphne, will not let me put her name with mine on the title page, saying that she has had little or nothing to do with this book. I disagree. But the only way to resolve matters is for me to dedicate it to her, with love.

PREFACE

THIS small book may seem superfluous in view of the excellent literature produced, especially of late, about the hereafter. I feel, however, that while some of these books err in being too scientific (and one cannot know man only through science) others are over-sentimental and indefinite. Some, too, are very abstract and philosophical and not sufficiently practical and mundane. Some, too, are written from the viewpoint of the psychologist and see any after-life as purely subjective, just as others ignore the riches which depth psychology has given us and consider matters as relating only to an external psychic world. And all this without taking into account those which are more or less heavily tainted with wishful thinking rather than being detached and objective. So this may serve as something intermediate between them all.

One thing which has become increasingly apparent while making this study is the singular unanimity which emerges from so many sources, if only in fragments. I will name only a few such as Professors H. Habberley Price of Oxford, and

C. D. Broad of Cambridge; psychologists of the stature of C. G. Jung; writers like Aldous Huxley: basically, and perhaps using different terms, they share a common view about man: though let it be added that they might repudiate this, just as they would probably refuse to agree to what I myself have written. But I feel, besides, that they also fall into line with tradition as found in ancient scriptures, among which pride of place may be given to the Tibetan and Egyptian Books of the Dead. I might add that among the many gaps in my own reading was that of Evans Wentz's edition of the Tibetan Book, the Bardö Thödol. It only came my way after I had written the first draft of this text. The reader can imagine my delight when I realized how near my own reflections had brought me to the ideas incorporated in it, as well as in the most valuable commentaries of the Tibetan translator, and of C. G. Jung, which are embodied in the volume.

I feel however that one must realize that all discussion of the deeper aspects of birth and death has to be looked on as speculative. Even the individual who speaks with most authority sees things only from a personal viewpoint, and it is likely that no two people will have the same experience except in general terms. On only one point can we be reasonably certain: that the one who goes through the gateway of death armed with road-map and timetable, believing he knows just what is going to happen to him, will have many surprises in store. Indeed, he may find himself more bewildered and at sea than the one who does not think he knows. One day we shall find out for ourselves. For the present, let us draw no hasty conclusions.

Thanks are due for criticism and help to many people unnamed: a hint here, a remark there, all contribute to the whole. But W. J. Ross, and Gwenyth and Warren Blakely, all of Ojai, California, worked through the early stages of my MS., sometimes dealing severely with me—which I deserved; and their criticisms helped a great deal. I am very grateful to them.

L. J. B.

I sometimes think of what kind Death will bring
When time's last knell has cut the tale of years,
And brought to close this little life.   No tears,
No bleak moth-fears besmirch her rainbow wing.
She comes, a quiet friend, to loose the cling
Of old grey hands upon a life that bears
No further fruit.   She ends a sleep and clears
The way—to what new freedoms? breaks the ring
Which prisons shining mind in grey-coiled brain;
Until, when earth-tinged thought has had its day,
In dawn-clear vision of God's face, by awe,
The tatters of this self are burned away.

Then, when time's inwound spool unfurls again,
'Tis Death who turns the soul to birth once more.

JOHN WESTERMAN

CONTENTS

INTRODUCTION

'What shall be the nature of our existence after death? The answer is found in the answer to another question: what is the nature of our existence now?... The secrets of the unknown are hidden in the known. The Kingdom is at hand, and death is neither its entrance nor its exit, but only an event we have met before.'

Harmon H. Bro, 'Four Paradoxes of Death,'
Inward Light, Vol. XXIV, No. 62

THE background of the chapters which follow is contained in the quotation above, and still more in the article from which it is taken. It suggests that the basis of life is in timeless and universal Being, which becomes projected for evolutionary purposes into the space-time world of *existence*.

Existence can only be significant when seen against its root in pure Being. Birth, growth, decay and death and, if the tradition be true, rebirth, are all part of a single process. They are, moreover, not separate parts, but each one co-exists all the time with the others, even when one aspect predominates.

The total process of existence is called evolution. In the words of Teilhard de Chardin it consists in the passage of Life from a primitive, ' Alpha ' state of minimal consciousness—better called preconsciousness—to an ' Omega ' state where consciousness, as understood by man today, reaches its zenith, after which it passes over into a new phase which, in the perennial philosophy of mankind, is often described as the extinction or void of Nirvana. Alpha, the first letter of the Greek alphabet is the beginning, Omega, the last letter, the end. Somewhere between them man appears, bringing with him the seed of individuality and of *self*-consciousness without which consciousness would not be able to differentiate itself from the massive yet vague and nebulous cloud of instinctive life, to become clear and focused as it must be in order to reach its conclusion. It is perhaps not too fanciful to suggest that this stage occurs roughly halfway through the alphabet, at Omicron. It is here that what Teilhard calls 'hominization', or 'becoming man', takes place; where a little self is born in order that it may grow and finally be transformed into the greater Self at the Omega point. The short-lived sound 'o' associated with omicron, as in '*on*' can legitimately be linked with the long-drawn 'Omega' in words like *cone*, as suggesting the relation of the two phases of self-identity, the personal and the spiritual, the former being a reflection into existence of the latter in the world of Being.

It is only against such a vast and awe-inspiring canvas that the various stages which seem so important in individual daily life can be evaluated and understood. These stages belong to the physical space-time world even when they pass beyond it; but this world is in fact a more or less illusory projection of eternal Reality. It belongs to the realm of what is in Sanskrit termed *māyā*, a concept which includes that of 'illusion' but which, paradoxically, sees that illusion as having pragmatic evolutionary value, and so as itself belonging to the world of the Real.

This pragmatic use of 'illusion' justifies the dissection of the total life-process as if the different phases were separate entities. For it enables us to place them side by side and so make it easier to reach the ' Gestalt ' which shows us the wholeness of life. But if one considers the puzzled, anxious individual, who may be driven to despair by events which seem to him overwhelming, he is entitled to what may be called first-aid, emergency treatment through some form of reassurance and comfort. By it he will not reach understanding of Truth. This he has to discover for himself; but while he is in a state of shock and distress, even a partial view may help to tide him over the emergency and may even be the starting point from which he can resume the quest for himself as he recovers.

The first proposition which can be put forward as especially applicable to the bereaved is that birth and death are entirely natural phenomena. One is essentially not a cause for rejoicing and the other equally not one for grief. I say ' essentially ' for both joy at the birth of a child and grief when a loved person vanishes from one's ken are also entirely natural human emotions and have to be accepted as such. Such, however, is human nature today that while birth is willingly faced and in fact idealized and sentimentalized, there

are many who refuse to look death in the face.
They fear it, they refuse to think of its inevitability,
they refer to it indirectly, saying 'If anything
happens . . .' rather than, ' When I die ', or ' When
X dies . . .' The person who is entirely philosophical about death, accepting it together with
the pain which goes with it for those left behind,
is still rare. Even the person who seems to have
evolved a precise belief as to the various phases
governing death and the hereafter, is often only
too blatantly hiding his fears under a faith which
may not outlast the time of fair weather before
he has to face what he thinks of as an ordeal.
Moreover, one thing seems likely: that the one
who starts on the journey beyond physical life
armed with timetable and road-map is probably
going to have more surprises and be far more
bewildered than the unthinking person passing into
that life without preconceptions as to the exact
pattern of things to come.

The reactions of the survivors of a death are
compounded of many things. There is the obvious
grief at losing a beloved presence, and this should
not be minimized. Few people are actually
' above such things ' and to suppress shock and
grief is to attempt to evade a situation which is

real. But there are times when somebody dies
and no emotion is consciously felt except perhaps
a sense of relief which makes the survivor feel
wicked and guilty. Under the relief there may
be genuine grief; yet to feel free from the slavery
of being tied to a person, especially after long
illness, the freedom many feel from domination of
even the most benevolent kind, the joy of being
now footloose in the world, are genuine and in
no way reprehensible when they occur. And if
a person has a real deep sense of the naturalness
of life's processes, there may really be no place in
them for a grief which would only be misplaced.

Normally, however, people feel the loss of a
beloved presence. At the personal level there is a
gap and, even apart from complications, this is a
sad and painful event. The pain should be recognized and accepted, not suppressed or evaded.
It is not only usual, it is perhaps an intrinsic aspect
of personal life, where happiness and pain both
belong and, moreover, are both creative experiences
if properly understood. I do not believe that even
the most genuinely spiritual and enlightened person
escapes. Indeed, because of his more sensitive
and acutely aware nature, I think that the saint
and the mystic probably experience suffering even

more deeply and intensely than the average man or woman. But he avoids the error of the average man, in that he does not identify and drown in that experience. He knows where it belongs, which part of him feels it, and that that part is not himself as a whole being. So he deals positively with it by his acceptance of it, by experiencing it to the very fullest extent and without resistance. This makes him free and, after a time, as the forces involved in the process expend themselves, he is healed of his wound.

There are other things which may cause pain at the sight of death. These are at once less direct and less obvious than the plain fact of loss. They stem from emotional involvement with the dead person: ' There, but for the grace of God, go I: I might be the dead man, I might be undergoing the ordeal of something I believe myself not to know,' and so on. ' And I might be like my friend, a failure: he, seen as myself, achieved no goal, no fulfilment. I have so far not completed what I believe to be my task in life. Were I cut off now, it would be before I did so, and the chance would have gone.' So the inner argument might go, valid except for the key fact that I am *not* the dead man and only feel myself to be so from projection of my own mental contents onto him, and identification with him. The same thing may happen if I feel guilty about my own moral state, and hence fear post-mortem retribution, if I fear the day when I shall come face to face with the inevitable, and so on. In other words, one can feel grief, not for the dead person, but self-pity or self-reproach projected onto him. One is sorry for oneself, not for him.

Many cases are compounded from these and other factors too individual and too personal to be gone into here. If one can understand just what one does feel, and why, the whole matter becomes stripped down to the primary and essential emotion of genuine and direct pain connected with the void in one's life: and that is definitely a passing thing, very different from the morbid and prolonged state of mourning which some people go through, almost as if they enjoyed it.

If we leave aside now the emotional problems connected with death, we still have the matter of a general and philosophical consideration of the whole matter of mortality itself. When a person leaves his body, does he, as a personality, survive? And does he remain in touch with those still in their bodies, or does he lose touch with them altogether? May it not be that the loss of contact is merely due to the limitation of our perception? It is to try and find answers to these questions that people sometimes turn to the churches, on the one hand, and to spiritualism on the other.

Both these approaches perform a useful function in their respective spheres, but they are orientated more towards giving comfort than towards finding out the truth. The churches ask for faith, for belief that the Deity knows best, and that all is well because He is in charge. The spiritualists give solace in purporting quite sincerely and honestly to give messages and communications which put the living in touch with the departed soul. But they rarely care for critical and analytical study of what they report, for when a clear mind is applied to the messages they rarely stand the test.

Parapsychology or psychical research, on the other hand, is strictly scientific, but it frustrates itself by this very fact. It demands evidence and proof of what can probably never be proved, at least on strictly scientific lines. In the medical field, that most human of studies, the wise realize that the *art* of medicine is quite as important as the science, and that sometimes the most successful physician is the one who is not particularly scientific but who has the art of diagnosing and of healing well developed. The old-fashioned country practitioner is often a far better doctor as far as his results are concerned than the highly qualified and scientific specialist or consultant.

This is not to deny the value of the scientific approach. It provides a solid and factual background to our thinking, but it leaves a vast gap in true understanding. Much of life (and death) cannot be confined within the data obtainable by exact science, if such still exists. Who, for instance, can give scientific criteria for the value of a work of art or the relation between people? The small-minded scientist is apt to call any discussion of such matters ' anti-science '. The wiser one realizes that science goes just so far in the understanding of life or the universe, but that the greater part goes far beyond the bounds of science into a realm which may be termed ' unscience ' but certainly not, when intelligently discussed, ' anti-science '. The minor scientist has all the attributes of the professional—as against the vocational—priest. He classifies as heresy all the things he cannot encompass within the limits of his mind or of a dogmatic scheme. What he fails to realize is that the objective scientific approach is an attribute of the mind itself, and when properly developed, can be applied to matters quite beyond the methodology of science, with just as much exactitude as to those where experiment and statistical approaches are possible.

Science today tends too much to think that it is the paramount authority in life and study. Hence the lesser scientists are apt to be smug and tiresome, becoming a new kind of clergy, patronising the 'unscientific' and assuming the mantles of both philosopher and priest. In other words, science can, in the hands of its lesser devotees fall into the category of idolatry so well described by Tillich when he speaks of the fallacy of giving absolute value to matters which are not absolute. The clear thinker today realizes how science has become to many the modern name for religion, and how, in the Tillich sense, it has usurped a supremacy which it does not have by right.

In the ensuing chapters, as much validity is allowed to 'unscientific' thought, provided it is not clouded by emotionalism and retains its objectivity, as to the scientific brand in the narrower sense. For, while science has not only opened up many fields of study hitherto closed, it has also, in the subjective sphere, given us the mental faculty of objective and scientific thought about the inside of things, in places which objective scientific method cannot touch. To call this ' anti-science ' is only justified where the ' scientific ' mind, evolved in the first place by strict external disciplines, but now able to be used beyond the reach of these disciplines, is not applied to the problem under scrutiny. On the other hand, if the objectivity learned from the application of scientific method is kept and carried into the subjective realm, a rich and rewarding field of speculation become available and carries a conviction which no mere external proof can do. The French, those people who claim to be particularly logical and clear-thinking, realize that *conviction in time*, or inner certainty, is of paramount value in making true judgments: in other words, without realizing it, they concede the importance of inner and ' unscientific ' evaluation, and make it the equal in personal life of the more strictly ' scientific ' and experimental approach.

In matters such as we shall discuss, a combination of both the scientific approach (not its method) and of inner feeling about things is the only way which is likely to be fruitful. It leaves room for speculation and, when emotionalism can be eliminated, for a form of self-validation of ideas and principles which no amount of parapsychology or other external science can ever approach. At the same time it removes the snare of wishful thinking. And it also makes room for the faculty of wonder. The truly creative mind realises that wherever one looks there is mystery, and that mystery is a field for growth-promoting exploration. To the one who knows this both birth and death are things which exist as parts of the scheme of things but, like other matters, they form part of a great Whole of which man can never know more than a fragment. There is great joy in increasing the size of that fragment by speculation and intuition. Such people realize that there is no final answer to the events and meaning of birth and death except that which they find out for themselves; and that when they have found an explanation it will still not be final, but leaves always further problems to be explored. It is no detriment that there is no proof of a scientific nature that man does not vanish as an individual when he leaves his body: they *know*, in a quiet yet unshakeable way that, whatever the individuality of each may eventually become, it is something which endures at least as long as the universe endures. The unsolved and perhaps insoluble question is the nature of this individuality when it reaches its fruition, and how this is to be achieved from the point where people stand today.

As against this, and contrary to what one might think at first, absolute certainty, the sense that everything is known which can be known, is frustrating and deadening. It removes any possibility of mental movement, it leaves no place for mystery and wonder, and so takes out from life the exercise of one part of the essential nature of man, curiosity. This attribute it is which makes him dynamic and urges him to expand always the frontiers of his field of knowledge, whether this knowledge has any practical value or not. Nobody can say that to climb an unconquered mountain adds except indirectly to man's useful knowledge (the indirect value being in the fields of psychology and physiology, not of geography) yet there are people to whom the very fact that there is an untrodden place is sufficient for them to risk their lives to get there. To dismiss such an adventurous spirit as merely showing off is not to do justice to the irrational sense that it is something to be pleased about, that it shows the 'manliness' of character of those who take the risks, and so on. There is human value in exploration for the sake of exploration, with utilitarian ends only secondary or remotely behind. On the other hand, when the summit is trodden, when the unknown has become known, there is often a certain flatness which follows the getting there.

Where the deeper aspects of human life are concerned, such flatness need never occur, for there is never a final answer to them. There are always further fields asking to be explored and understood. This is very much the case with life and death. We see certain things, we obtain certain evidence, we think some things probable and others not. But the mystery which surrounds us on every side is not lifted anywhere, it is only pushed a little further away as the mind extends outward into the unknown, and rejoices in having this unknown into which to grow. No final answers can be offered as to the phenomena or the meaning of life and death. So, though it would be tedious to begin each suggestion in the chapters which follow with a caution that ' It seems as if . . .', this tentativeness should always be read into any seemingly categorical statements we make.

1

THE CONSTITUTION OF MAN

BEFORE going on to considering the matter of death and dying, it will be well to have some idea of the structure of the only creature in the natural world to whom they are a problem, and why this is so. The pre-human animal does not theorize. He lets himself be carried easily and happily by the rhythms of nature, and because he does not resist them, there is no conflict. Man on the other hand does resist, and this both sets up conflict and shows him to be different from the animal. He either has something more or something less than the animal. Indeed he has both more and less. What is added to him is the power of theorizing and of considering things both before and after they have happened. This robs him of the spontaneity and directness of response to events as they happen. He thinks, and, in so doing, he wraps himself up in a cocoon of ideas, associations and memories, so that when something occurs he is only too often confused and unable to act directly, but automatically calls up previous experiences and what he thinks he has learned from them. This veils the novelty of the moment which, however much it may resemble other and previous similar moments is nevertheless different from every past event, if only by the passage of time.

This propensity has certain advantages from the evolutionary and survival point of view, but it can also stand between the forward-moving and therefore truly creative response which can be seen at times in simple animals and young children, but rarely in adult life.

It is due essentially to the fact that human beings are individuals and animals are not. Animals belong to a group and are, except in the case of the highest domestic animals, governed by the mass consciousness of that group. Man is, very evidently if we watch our fellows and ourselves, still very much at the mercy of mass consciousness, especially at the emotional and instinctive level; but within that ocean there is in every human being the germ of a unique and discrete selfhood. The purpose of human evolution is to develop that selfhood and bring it to fruition, just as in the next lower kingdom, that of the animal, the purpose of life appears to be to bring the evolving life to the point where individuality comes into it if only as a potentiality.

This is recognized, though perhaps not directly, by such writers as Teilhard de Chardin in his already quoted study of *The Phenomenon of Man*. He realizes, however, that man, as a physical organism, is weaker, more vulnerable and in many ways inferior to the lower animals; but, as some animals develop claws and teeth, or speed of motion, or protective colouring, or horny carapaces as a means of survival, man's means of finding safety for himself lies not in improved physical organs and mechanisms, but in a sphere altogether new in evolution. This he calls the *noosphere* or sphere of knowledge, reason and mind. It appears to be this, and the fact that he is developing the equipment to make it active, which makes man what he is, the most creative and destructive as well as the most powerful creature on earth.

If we study his mind, however, we find there all the animal mentality, instincts, and the perceptive

powers which the animal uses extensively in hunt-
ing and escaping, and in many other ways; but
in the centre of it is the core of identity, of
conscious selfhood. There may be such identity
or selfhood in the animal, but it is evident that
this lies not so much within each individual as in
the species or sub-species to which it belongs. It
is more a foreshadowing than an actuality. Not
only is each individual animal body directly conditioned to behave according to mass instinctive
patterns which govern collective behaviour, but it
also seems to call sometimes for the ' sacrifice '
of that body where it serves the welfare of the
herd or group. It is not an act of individual
heroism on the part of the bee which kills itself
by stinging, or even of the defenders of a herd of
buffalo or elephants, but an entirely natural and
unconsidered action in the face of danger. It is
directed at helping the survival and safety of the
group as a whole.

Man, however, tends automatically to think
first of himself and of his own safety, only after-
wards of others. The more ' civilised ' he is, up
to a certain point, the more obvious is this selfish
tendency. On each side of a certain critical point
of maximum individualism in civilisation there is on

the primitive side the tendency for a tribe or clan to act as a whole and for the individual to be subordinated and sacrificed to the general welfare; while on the other side of that point there is increasingly a self-chosen sense of duty towards one's fellows, even at the cost of life itself. The action is the same, the motivating power is different. In the first instance the individuality is weak and still deeply embedded in its animal heritage of instinct and mass response, in the second it is due to transcendence of what is, in effect, a first stage of individual self-assertion where ' I ' comes first and others are of only secondary importance. The fact of individuality is, however, predominant at all stages. It is as he grows that man's idea of that individuality changes.

At this point Hindu philosophy provides an important key. It calls the ' I-making faculty ' *ahamkara*, and considers it as the basic human attribute. There are many shades of meaning to this word. Some, the Vedantins, take it as running right through the human constitution from the principle which is, into that personal reflection of the spiritual man, which EXISTS. They even sometimes substitute Ahamkara for the term *Atma* or *Atman*, the very highest human principle, coupling it with Buddhi and Manas as the spiritual trinity in man on the one hand, and with *Brahman*, the supreme Deity on the other. The Buddhists and other Hindu groups look on it differently, and, as Monier Williams tells us, restrict it to the *conception*, not to the *ultimate reality*, of one's individuality or self-consciousness: a 'false' image, which, as in every religion, has to be discarded before entering *Nirvana*, the Kingdom, *Moksha*, liberation, or whatever we may choose to call it—a state of pure *Being*, no longer *existence* or 'standing outside'. If this is realized it explains the paradoxes which tell us that we have to 'lose our life in order to find it', that we have to 'forget the self', and so on.

In any case, it seems unlikely that if the whole of evolution has worked on an aeonian scale towards the establishment of self-identity, this has to be discarded rather than changed and transformed, as is the custom in all natural processes, as the evolutionary wave proceeds. It seems therefore that we can assume that some form of self persists as man goes on to transcend manhood, and that in the spiritual realm of Being he is still him-Self though he may be stripped of the outer husks of the selfhood he knows in his personal, existential life, and which, for most of us, most of the time, is what we refer to as ' I '.

If, then, we take man to be Self in a way the animal is not, we can go on to consider in detail the two main aspects of his being, the spiritual, and the personal; and, following Saint Paul, to divide the latter into body (*soma*) and soul (*psyche*) or mind; both being existential reflections of *Pneuma* or the spirit, which is, and only (to use inadequate language) fragmentarily incarnates into the world of activity in space-time. It is important, however, that despite the dissection which follows, we always remember the unity of what is in effect the field in which the total man works. Just as a wheel only remains a wheel so long as axle, spokes, felloes and rim form an integral whole, so it is with man. In more modern terms of ' field theory ' man is a ' standing wave pattern ' undergoing constant growth and development. The pattern makes him ' objective ' in the world of *things*, and it derives its form from an immense complexity of forces and energies playing into one another from all levels, spiritual, psychic and physical. The divisions we are going to make are therefore in a sense artificial and must not be taken as real so much as convenient. In any case, as we shall hope to show, there are no sharp lines of demarcation between one aspect and the other, but they overlap and so, in function, fade into one another by an infinite number of gradations. Man, mathematically considered, is an integral equation of the calculus, not a differential one; yet, as mathematicians know, the differential calculus is a necessary complement to the integral.

2

THE BODY

It is generally assumed that the body is a solid, material object, behind which lies directly the soul or spirit. Ancient tradition, however, confirms what clairvoyants have described, which is that the living body is a dual structure, part material in the sense that it consists of solids, liquids and gases, part vital consisting of an interweaving of streams of energy, or in Sanskrit, *prana*, where the general field of prana is subdivided into ten *vayus* or 'vital airs' each having a distinct function in the whole. The Egyptians, among others, believed in the *kaa* or subtle counterpart of the body, and took steps to preserve it through its connection with the physical form. The Tibetans too have a similar tradition. It is often referred to in modern literature on the occult, as the etheric or vital body.

Science has so far paid little attention to this aspect of matter, but of late years more and more work has been done in the field of electricity where, by modern electronic methods, it is possible to detect minute variations in the electrical potential of different parts of the body, not only of animals but in all living matter. These methods also allow records to be made of oscillations in the field, so that tracings are made not only of the relatively large electrical phenomena connected with the heart-beat, but the much subtler ones of the brain itself, where no part of the tissues moves as does the heart muscle. In the latter, the state of consciousness of the subject show consistent variations when read on the electro-encephalogram. Interest, emotional disturbance, sleep, hypnosis, active perception of external events, all show distinct patterns; whereas disease in the brain or nervous system can sometimes be detected before any clinical manifestations occur.

Out of these discoveries theoretical considerations emerge, and there is a distinct movement towards the view that living bodies differ from dead ones in the fact that there is an electrical field which determines the livingness of a certain collection of chemical atoms, and that when that field disappears or disintegrates, the organism breaks up into smaller components and reverts to ' dust '. Indeed, the use of radio-isotopes goes so far as to suggest that what is stable and enduring while a body is alive is not the solid matter of which tissues are made, but the field into which that material as it were silts, in order to create a living organism. It gathers together in increasing quantities as growth proceeds, yet it does not, as one might imagine, stay where it is, but actually flows through the field in a constant stream. Thus an atom of radio-active iodine or iron may be found at one time in one organ but a short while later in another, perhaps fulfilling a different function in a new combination with other elements. Heraclitus' dictum that ' Panta rhei ', ' everything is in flux ' applies here in a marked and unexpected way.[1]

Extending the material available and bringing together various aspects of the question, it seems as if the body is a highly complex system of different energies. Some of these, which we shall call chemical, are those of the atoms of which the tissues are made, and the electro-magnetic fields between them. This is in line with modern science and, moreover, applies to the inorganic

[1] See The Science Group Journal, Theosophical Research Centre, London, Feb. 1963.

matter at the chemical and physical levels as much as to that of organic living bodies. But where we have living beings, there is another set of energies which are ' vital ' and determine whether a certain accumulation of atoms be living or not. Moreover, while some of these energies appear to act regardless of consciousness, others respond to the influence of thought and feeling. In this way the vital energy-field becomes subdivided into the truly *sub*conscious, which governs the vegetative aspects of life: digestion, temperature, metabolic regulation and the like; and those associated with directed and purposeful thought and feeling at a higher level than the vegetative life, whether the activity of this level be conscious or *un*conscious (without of necessity being *sub*conscious).

Life depends on an interplay between the chemical and the vital energy-fields, each one influencing the other, so that there is an overall pattern in living organisms while they are alive. In disease, the harmonious interplay is locally disorganized. At death, the two fall apart entirely.

What happens to the chemical components of the total field is well enough known and fairly obvious. But what happens to the vital and psychologically governed aspect is scientifically a matter of conjecture in which any view, from that of its dissolution at the moment of physical death which represents one extreme, and its persistence for an indefinite time the other.

The vital or bio-electrical field, however, is clearly physical. It acts at its most material levels in and between the atoms; at the intermediate stage it governs autonomic bodily economics and works through the sympathetic and parasympathetic nervous systems and through its effects on the chemical-secreting endocrine glands. The key point of these in the anatomy of the body is the hypothalamus, and the pituitary gland which is associated with the hypothalamus in the brain. The higher levels, associated with psychic activity, however, express themselves through the cerebrospinal nervous system, using it as the vehicle for conveying the impulses which make up physical awareness and activity, to and from the inner focus of the individual where consciousness resides.

The vital field is, however, not itself conscious: it is the carrier of consciousness in the same way as a nerve carries impulses without itself being sensitive to the message it conveys. A nerve fibre can be manhandled in surgery without any pain or other sensation in that patient unless, by some chance, it is stimulated so that an impulse passes up it to the cell body in the spinal cord or brain which is the place of origin of the fibre. That stimulus is then translated into vision in the case of nerves associated with the retina, sound with those from the ear, and so on, without the original cause of the impulse being in any way connected with light or noise. The nature of what ' I ' become aware of, depends on the function of the nerve, on it being set into action, and not on the external circumstances which may or may not have stimulated the actual sense organ to which the nerve runs. Give an electrical stimulus to the optic nerve and light is perceived, to the auditory nerve and sound is heard, to a fibre concerned with temperature, and heat or cold are noted. In other words, the function of a nerve fibre is automatic, and ' unconscious ' even though it carries messages to and from consciousness. In the same way, the general vital field will convey information to the conscious centre of the individual during life but it is not itself conscious. It is a bridge mechanism. If it should hold together after death it will have become the ' outermost ' sheath or vehicle of the man-within, though removed from its entanglement with the chemical bodily field.

An interesting matter has been found out in connection with the body as known to the individual. It is called the ' body image ' and is known to psychologists and neurologists because of the persistence of a certain sense of bodily pattern in people who have been injured either in brain or limb. Normally, we are unaware of this body image. But when something goes wrong with the body, we still tend unconsciously to refer to what has become impressed on the mind by force of habit. Thus a person who has lost a leg has to undergo a process of re-education before he ceases to 'feel' that limb as if it were still there physically, one who has had muscles transplanted to restore function after ' polio ' has to learn how to make the muscles work so as to bend the elbow, let us say, where previously they extended it.

Tradition, where it is explicit, leads us to think that that ' body image ' tends to persist for a time at least after there is no body to cause it. The result is that a newly ' dead ' person, if he is in any way conscious, tends to carry with him the habit of a lifetime and, for some while does not realise that he is dead as far as the physical world is concerned. This is reflected in all religions where prayers are said for the departed, and certain rituals performed around their bodies. Basically these are aimed at allowing the soul to move away, and to remove him from any possible distress at seeing his erstwhile home decaying or being burned on a pyre. Even where, as in orthodox Christianity, the simple desire to free the soul has become coupled with more complex and less realistic prayers for a salvation which perhaps the dead person has not immediately deserved, the tradition still exists.

Occult lore suggests that this stage of unbelief in the fact that one is no longer in a body lasts a matter of a few days, though it allows that it may be extended or shortened under special circumstances. These circumstances depend on the state of mind of the individual, not on what is done with the body or, ultimately, for the soul of the departed if he should be too in-turned to be accessible to outside influences. We need therefore to consider now the next level of the human being, his soul or psyche; since that is the operative field in which *human* evolution takes place. But in order to understand this it will be more practical to discuss, as far as one can discuss the transcendental, the aspect of man which is the polar opposite of the body, the spirit.

3

THE SPIRIT

In principle, spirit cannot be defined directly, for whatever is said about it is of necessity only partly true and may have to be complemented by another statement which perhaps contradicts the previous one. The reason for this is that man's mind has evolved from the simple, practical level of animal mentality, but that it is far short of what it can eventually become. Hence man's perceptions and his ability to understand, are adequate for the past, and for those levels of evolution he has already been through. It has not yet developed the potentialities which belong to his future. That is why the spirit is to him the great unknown, the place of paradox, of contradiction, of non-sense which is a deeper reality and truth than anything he can learn through his senses and his sensible mind.

Man has, in the course of endless evolutionary ages, come to the place where his sense of individuality is firmly established. It is true that this focus of self often gets carried away in the torrent of mass hysteria, mass behaviour, mass desires, but it nevertheless survives and is the growth-point of understanding. From it he can look back into the past, in order to anticipate on the line of causality the future; he can cogitate and reflect and theorize about life. But he works within a limited horizon beyond which lies the mystery of the unknown. Spirit lies beyond this horizon, unseen except by the few who have learned to lift their awareness from the evolutionary place they are in, and so see further than most people in their normal state. They are the yogis, the saints, the seers, the mystics, some of whom appear to have achieved a state of being which puts them outside the run of the ordinary man. The latter, however, often has his own moments of vision, sometimes under most unexpected circumstances, when he is in the deepest despair or pain, or in the ecstasy of love, or of seeing or hearing the inner beauty of a work of true art, but then he falls back again to his normal, or, to be more exact, to a new normal, but still mundane level of life; for experience of a spiritual nature inevitably leaves the beholder or partaker somehow changed for what we call the better. This change is, indeed, the test of what has been experienced, differentiating it from an emotional occurrence which, once it has passed its peak, leaves him much where he was before, perhaps even with a sense of flatness and frustration due to the slackening of the tension he has felt during the experience itself.

Something of the nature of spirit can be derived theoretically if we think of it as in every way the opposite of the material body, and hence as having contrary attributes. The body, meshed into natural time, with its cyclic quality, is definitely mortal. The spirit can be defined as that which is beyond time and hence is immortal (though it must be added that its timelessness may be only freedom from the tyranny of time as we know it, since there may be other forms and dimensions of time of which we are as yet entirely unaware). The body is limited and circumscribed, located in space: spirit is unlimited and hence universal, with the same qualification as to universality as applies to time. The body, as it improves, throughout animal evolution, increasingly refines, elaborates, and becomes able to focus its perceptive organs more and more closely. It can therefore see more and more differentiation in the world it lives in. Spirit is unfocused, unlocalized, all-embracing, hence concerned with generalities and principles, for which reason its consciousness is often called ' cosmic ' or ' eternal ', in contrast to what we know of the material world.

Now, however, we come to what is perhaps the most important difference between physical and spiritual awareness. While in the physical world we have to exclude in order to study in detail a certain object or subject. The spirit, by virtue of its very inclusiveness, is able to see detail and wholeness at the same time. Through the detailed and the minute it sees the universal, but equally, from the universal it knows the detailed. This almost incomprehensible fact calls out such para-doxical sayings as ' seeing the world in a grain of sand and eternity in an hour ' (or, in modern terms, the cosmos in an electron and eternity in a fraction of a second: the electron being taken as the smallest particle of what we call matter, while the fraction of a second is in reality the shrunken instant we call the ever-evanescent and durationless present).

It is only by constantly teasing the mind with these contradictions that anything of the nature of spirit can be understood from ' below ', at the psychic level. The fact that even so much can be understood, however, is because the psyche is itself included in the spiritual nature and partakes of it, as we shall see later.

To the western mind, spirit is therefore usually seen as something undifferentiated within itself, a ' moreness ' we sometimes speak of simply as God. As we have said—and the inadequacy of words is most apparent—it IS and does not *exist*; and yet existence, like mayavic ' illusion ', is an aspect of the totality of Being and hence of Reality. In the East, however, and particularly in Hindu-Buddhist philosophy, it is more explicitly described. Just as in Christianity, and particularly in the Athanasian Creed, the Godhead is defined as a Trinity and great effort is made to show how this Trinity is yet a unity and that none is " before or after ", superior or inferior to the other aspects, so is the spirit described in the East. The true Self of man is said to *be* the Ātman and to *exist* as *Ātma, Buddhi* and *Manas*.

Ātma or the Ātman corresponds to the Father aspect of the divine Trinity, and is said to be the source of all conscious being, unity with which is the purpose and goal of human evolution. In

Christianity we speak of ' sitting on the right hand
of the Father ', of ' being hid with Christ in God '
and in other ways indicate this ultimate goal. The
' Christ ' or Son aspect, which, be it noted, is to
be ' with us ' when we become ' hid in God ',
is Buddhi.

The latter is as difficult to comprehend in
ordinary language as is Ātma. It is said to be
the ' highest ' or most spiritual level at which
duality exists, Ātma being one only. The paradox
of the Son aspect of the Trinity applies here, for
He is said to be ' true God and true man ' at once.
Buddhi, as experienced, seems to have this duality,
in that it both perceives and acts, through the
personal levels of man. Its perception is in itself
dual as it brings about an act of ' knowing ' which
is beyond and involves no ordinary mental action
such as that we ordinarily use. Professor Ernest
Wood says that this form of knowing is more like
pure and direct cognition than it is like thought;
and, indeed, that thought only gets between the
knower and the knowing. It is a complete understanding of both the whole of an object and of its
parts, and of its relation to the greater whole in
which and by which it exists. It is illumination. On
the feeling side which accompanies the illumination

there is intense feeling but no such movement as the word ' emotion ' indicates. It is ecstatic, giving a sense of reality and wonder which is beyond any ordinary affective experience, hence it is often referred to as ' bliss '. The two aspects, the understanding or knowing, and the feeling, are inextricably interwoven.

Manas, unqualified, is a word having the same root as our own ' man ' and ' mind ', is pure, *unconditioned* mind. The ordinary workaday mind is always much conditioned by memory, association, and the feelings which belong to these, but manas, in a strange way, though it is the instrument of all action, mental or physical, in the first instance, appears to be completely inactive in its pure state. It springs into activity only when stimulated by Buddhi, when it acts in a direct manner, from with-in, and not as where *kama* or instinct is active. Stimulated by kama it behaves reactively to conditions, memories, and other stimuli belonging to the more material levels of existence. Pure manas is poised and still, as the centre of a circle is still, the hub of a wheel is immobile while the rim spins. This quality is hinted at, though rarely if ever explicitly described when it is equated with the ' point within a circle from which every part of the circumference is equidistant ', in the ' Middle Way ' of the Buddhist and in any other image which suggests stillness or balance or a ' nothing-ness ' which is also ' everythingness '.

Manas activated by Buddhi is the ' higher ' or illumined mind, and is paired with its reflection into the psychic and personal levels as Kāma-Manas, or the ' lower ' mind, of which we shall speak later. In this way, the third aspect of spirit can be looked upon as the inactive focus from which all personal activity springs, the nature of that activity being determined by which aspect of the feeling life, the spiritual Buddhi or the psychic, personal, or kamic, is the motivating force.

Spirit is further equated with selfhood. As we have already said, Hindu philosophy sometimes places Ahamkāra, or ' I-am-ness ' where others speak of Ātma. In other writings, Manas-in-action is equated with self-identity, but here the reference is to the form of I-ness which is our personal and conscious focus, and is of quite a different kind from spiritual identity and its qualities. Ordinary personal I-ness is separative, discrete, divisive, whereas the I-ness of spirit is based on the paradoxical state of being at once completely one-Self and at the same time one with every other creature.

This principle gives validity to the notion of spiritual ' life eternal ' for every human being, and to its only being reached when personal, separative selfhood is transcended and transformed. It suggests that in the early stages, *ahamkāra* is in the position of an embryo which can only develop when enclosed and separated from its environment by the amnionic membrane, but that sooner or later it can only go further when it divests itself from these membranes, emerges naked from the shell which has so far been ' itself '. Another analogy is where an insect larva ' dies ' as it becomes a chrysalis, resolving itself into what is almost a dead organism, only to revive in a new form and emerge as the imago or full-fledged insect.

This brings with it the suggestion that what we know as ' I ' in our ordinary psychic and physical life can be looked on as a reflection, a lower harmonic, of the true spiritual identity. The development of that ' lower ' self is a manifestation of spirit, it is the focus from which all growth takes place. It is achieved only as a climacteric in evolutionary history, but, when it has served its purpose, it needs to be transformed—not killed out—as man becomes liberated from mere humanity and passes on into whatever lies beyond. As Nietzsche said in his *Zarathustra*, man is a transition, a means and not an end, and the glory of him is that as he fulfils himself as man he destroys himself by his own act.

4

THE SOUL

THE word " soul " is commonly used in a number
of different ways. This makes it unsatisfactory
and tends to confusion. It is often taken as the
synonym of spirit, whereas at other times it is made
to refer to some rather indefinite aspect of man's
non-physical being. It is in fact the English
equivalent for the Greek *psyche*, which refers to
something less concrete than *soma* or dense body,
and yet more personal than *pneuma*, or spirit-in-
action (hence the use of the same word as for
' breath ') or *nous*, spirit as the knower or perceiver.
It is also equivalent to the word ' mind ', but this
word is of little help since to some it stands for the
thinking principle only (*manas*) and to others, the
majority, for the totality of the thinking-feeling
aspect of man (*kāma-manas*). For these reasons,

we shall use the word *psyche* in much the same way as it is used in current psychology, to cover all that part of man which is neither physical nor the spirit, and so, as inclusive of all the ' mental ' functions.

It is a convenient word too in that it resolves the division to be found in some theosophical books, as also in the teachings of Gurdjieff, where we are told of a series of distinct ' bodies ' (in Sanskrit, *koshas* or, with a shade of meaning different from this, *upadhis*) in one of which we experience thought, in another feeling or emotion, and so on. The correspondence with the Sanskrit terms is, let it be said, loose; but the same idea pervades the notion of psychic and even spiritual " bodies " as is in the Indian words, of their being ' vestures ' of the spiritual essence of man, the Ātman, through which it experiences in various ways.

For our purposes, the psyche is that part of man in which he thinks and feels on the one hand, cognizes or perceives on the other. It is also the place where he is normally aware of himself as ' I '. The idea of this as a body or bodies has a certain validity in that a ' standing wave pattern ', such as a beam of light, can be said to have a certain shape, a certain extension in space and time. But the more modern outlook which thinks less in terms of objects with a more or less static outline, size, duration, and replaces this by the sense of things, even at the physical level as being dynamic, fields of energies intermingling and often in a constant state of change and flux, fits in much better with the characteristics of the psyche. The physical body can be to some extent stilled, though the breath, the circulation of blood and many other functions operate even when the whole organism is quiet. The thinking-feeling aspect of man as a whole, unlike the dense body, is in constant total movement, as everyone knows who has tried to concentrate or meditate. Indeed, the mind cannot be stilled without vanishing entirely, just as a flame, however steady, is really in perpetual movement until it ' goes out ', and so ceases to exist.

This concept may seem heresy when we read in books on meditation and yoga that the mind should be stilled. Yet it seems as if what is meant is a withdrawal of attention from the busy-ness of the mind rather than a deadening of its activity. It is quite possible to ignore this activity, if only for a few seconds at a time. But, just as the heart

goes on beating when attention is directed elsewhere, so does the psyche carry on its own motion,
in this instance truly *sub*consciously, while ' I ' may
be engaged in deep contemplation of things outside
and beyond the psychic field itself. The act of
' stilling ' is like the movement of a person from
the rim or spokes of a turning wheel to the centre
of that wheel. There he would be at rest even
while the rotation went on.

An important fact is that while thought and
feeling can be *conceptually* separated, they are
functionally indivisible. There is no thought without
some feeling, no feeling without thought also.
True, thinking, as for instance in higher mathe-
matics, can be almost without emotion: but even
then the thinker feels interest or pleasure in his
work; and one cannot feel emotion in a void, and
otherwise than *about* something, however vague
the thought. This chimes in with the ancient
tradition relating to the principles of man, as it
does with the knowledge of modern psychology,
in a far better way than with the idea of there
being a mental ' body ' separate from an emotional
or astral ' body '. A useful analogy for the two
functions is that thought is like the drawing in
a picture, feeling is the colour. One never exists

without the other. Even a ' black and white ' mechanical drawing cannot ever be pure black and pure white because the paper is slightly tinted, the ink not entirely opaque, the light by which it is seen a compound of hues. In the same way even the most abstract picture, consisting of blobs of colour or merging figures, is nevertheless contained within a frame, while the coloured patches also have some kind of shape however indefinite. So is it with all mental, or psychic, activity.

This means that every mental act is dual at least; and indeed, the psyche itself seems to be in every way a dual field, with the energies which create it and give it relative consistency coming from both ' ends ' or poles of the human field, the spirit and the earthy animal body. These can also be thought of as coming the one from within, the other from outside, the important point being that they are polar opposites, and hence complementary to one another.

The dual pull as between the instinctive, animal side of man and his spiritual aspirations becomes obvious to any reasonably introspective person. He soon discovers that his thoughts run between extremes in which some are entirely selfish, serving purely personal desires, while others can be truly idealistic, religious, aspiring, and self and its desires do not mar their quality. For the most part, of course, they are in a middle range where both aspects combine to make for something which is at once impersonal and yet gratifies the personality and its desires.

It should be added that this refers to true idealism, not to that which, outwardly unselfish, camouflages deep self-interest, the search for kudos and social or pseudo-spiritual advancement.

The ego or focus of ' I-ness ' can be considered as the focal point of the psyche. It is the growing-point of the human being, surrounded by a field of consciousness in which we are normally aware of what is going on around us. This field fades gradually into a dimmer and less conscious region, the personal unconscious, and this in turn merges into the general, collective unconscious. It is probable that in the most primitive man there is virtually no difference between the personal and the collective unconscious, or for that matter, between the conscious and unconscious personal fields. This only differentiates as thought develops, when, bit by bit, the personal and the collective on the one hand, the conscious and personal unconscious on the other, become to some degree separated from one another by what Professor Assagioli of Florence describes as a 'semi-permeable membrane'.

Assagioli's picture of the psyche is worth examining. It is in line with the basic pattern of every 'monad', be this an atom, a man, a solar system or a galaxy. Each has a centre, a field around it, and then some kind of limit—not always very apparent—a 'Ring-pass-not', to use a term found in the literature of occultism—separating it from a realm outside it. Within the field is an organized system of functions in which are included endless lesser monads, while every monad is itself contained within a greater monadic unit. Thus the chemical atom is within a molecule, a molecule can be in a cell, a cell in a body, a body in a greater, perhaps planetary, unit, the planet in a solar system. And each unit, however great or small, is part of and exists only by reason of an interplay with the other monads in and around it. In the case of the human psyche, it is clearly an entity within the total human field; each man is part of mankind, and cannot exist in complete isolation.

The picture Assagioli gives us is taken from the living organic cell. This has a nucleus, the personal ego. It is surrounded by a field of consciousness extending into the unconscious. Around this still personal area there is the collective, sometimes described as a ' plane ', astral or mental, or, better, astro-mental. This ' plane ' covers whatever wave-lengths or energy-levels are represented in thinking and in feeling emotion. The personal psychic field is separated from the collective by a semi-permeable membrane such as we find, let us say in a single yeast cell or an amoeba. It is semi-permeable in that the contents of the environing ' collective ', the medium in which the cell lives, filters into the cell body, while the contents of that cell body seep through into the surrounding fluid; so each affects the composition of the other.

If we consider man, this is precisely his own condition at the psychic level, receiving from and himself contributing to, the psychic world in which he lives, separated from it to some degree, but only able to survive because he is at once partly isolated but also partly connected and therefore nourished by it.

Assagioli, further adds both the body at one ' end ' of the psyche, and, more important, the centre of identity we call the Self at the other.

He sees this Self as at once the source of the personal ego which is a reflection of it within the psyche, and as itself standing, as it were, on the borderline between the psyche and the greater Self of collective Life, by whatever name it is known.

In man the conscious field surrounding the personal ego can be equated with that part of the total field which the physical brain can convey into physical waking consciousness at any one time. It is not a rigidly fixed area but more like the circle of light cast by a spotlight, which remains roughly the same in size wherever it moves. Whenever we move away from clear physical consciousness, as in sleep or in the state known as ' hypnogogic ', between sleep and full wakefulness, or in the half-way condition of mediumship, the field widens and also tends to lose its clear outline and focus, including more of the unconscious temporarily within its bounds.

The ego-nucleus can conveniently be thought of as standing between the physical brain-consciousness and the deeper or higher Self. It is at once the link and the obstruction between the two. Like the Roman god Janus, who stood at the city gates, with one face turned inward towards the town and one outwards to the countryside, it functions in one aspect in the direction of earth and desire, in the other towards spirit. In its early stages, just as a plant has to grow downwards and establish firm roots in the soil, it ignores the spiritual aspects of life and works vigorously in the field of animal life, instinct, self-preservation, self-enlargement and enrichment. This is for man the ' path of outgoing ' of the Hindu, represented in the Judaeo-Christian mythos in the persons of Adam and Eve and their immediate descendants after the " fall " into incarnation. It is only later, when physical life is secure, and supported by a considerable body of mental construction in the form of laws and institutions, that there is a turning towards the more spiritual aspect of things: the individual enters the ' path of return ' and Adam becomes the Prodigal Son.

It is at this period—and it is rarely merely a moment in time—that the ego-centre in the psyche, and the psyche as a whole, enters a long period of internal stress, one part warring against the other, selfishness conflicting with an impersonal sense of the need to sacrifice oneself for the benefit of others. Previously, the conflict had been between ' me ' and ' the other fellow ', now it is between ' I ' and ' me ' as well, ' I ' being the spiritual Self, ' me ' the personal or psychic reflection of that Self.

So a duality which may have been latent becomes actual in the life of the intelligent man and woman, and the ' ills of civilisation ' or living together with others beset us.

In view of the genetics, so to speak, of the psyche, as child of a spiritual father and an earthy mother, it is not surprising if, wherever and however we look at it, duality pursues us. It does not of necessity follow that the polarity is always, by analogy, vertical, between spirit and body, for, as in electro-magnetic phenomena, fields of force and energy can be induced at right angles to the original. It is well known that a magnetic field caused by the passage of an electrical current in a coil is at ninety degrees to the direction of flow of the current, and conversely if an electrical current is generated between the poles of a magnet. So does it seem to be with the psyche.

Jung has given us a classical description of the functions of the mind on the cognitive side, speaking of four functions which are respectively intuition, thought, feeling and sensation. These he arranges on a diagram where thought and feeling are diametrically opposed, and intuition and physical sensation form a complementary pair at the other cardinal points of the compass. In our book, *The Psychic Sense* (2nd edition) we have modified the original version by considering that there is a complete functional link between thought and feeling, on the one hand, and between intuition and physical sensation on the other. In this we can envisage what is inevitably the case, that every mental act within the confines of the psyche is a compound of thought and feeling in different proportions, and so can be ' placed ' anywhere between the ends of the axis of the *reflective function*. In like manner, the function of *perceptivity* runs from pure illumination to pure physical sensation through the body, combining in any act of cognition varying proportions of illumined intuitive knowledge with some degree of expression in terms of physical world perception. In practice, as we have repeatedly said, thought and feeling are always mixed, whereas no physical object is truly understood unless there is some degree of intuitive enlightenment, if only in a minute dose; while unless some fragment of a moment of pure enlightenment becomes translated, however haltingly, into language and physical symbols, it remains subjective, ' unearthed ' and, because of its very nature, inclined to overwhelm the one who experiences it and to loosen his hold on day to day realities.

If then we think of the psyche as a whole, it is evident that both perceptivity and reflection play a part in every act, if only indirectly. One may, for instance, be engaged in deep meditation on a problem. But the meditation, unless it be of the very high type, ' without seed ' of thought or object, (when it ceases from being a truly psychic activity) is *about* something, or some person, or some quality. Careful consideration will show us that, somehow, images related to objects mingle with the abstraction and give it form. These images may be drawn from memory of things seen or otherwise experienced even if not actually present at the moment. Likewise, perception of an object draws on the same fund of memory and association stored in the mind, in order to relate it to other things and so make it comprehensible. In other words, both reflection and perceptivity mingle constantly in much the same way as thought and feeling themselves.

By analogy the two functions may be said to be the warp and weft of the fabric of life. Where the threads cross is the point where the conscious self is at any moment of time. If we like, we can then put memory as a place where experience is stored in the background of active psychic life, in another dimension behind the living fabric, a source on which ' I ' can draw in trying to relate things to one another.

This consideration may seem somewhat abstract and to have little practical value, but it shows the complexities involved in even the simplest psychic act. It also shows that whatever we perceive is apt to be coloured by past experience, and not seen directly in its immediacy; that is, in the present instant and uncontaminated by what has gone before or by ideas of what is to come, or by predilections, prejudices and other conditioning factors. In this way each experience becomes tied to time past and future at the expense of the present where alone it actually makes its impact directly on the observing ego. There will be more to say about this as we go on.

Yet another duality in the psyche is represented by the two modes of action, the one receptive and perceptive, the other outgoing and active. The first is the system by which impacts from the outer world—physical, psychic or spiritual—reach the inner knower and, consciously or unconsciously, are there registered. The other is the mechanism by which the psyche causes action in its environment. Clearly, these are processes working in opposite directions, the one from outside in, the other from inside outward.

A very usual process is that the ego or knower receives impulses from the outside world and sends out appropriate stimuli to bring about a certain reaction. A man sees a snake, thinks it poisonous, and jumps back at once. At a more abstract level somebody says something which he dislikes, and he answers by a wounding repartee, or he reads opinions which do not appeal to him and his mind hardens up against the disturbance to his mental peace. In other words, there is an interim between receipt of external information and reaction to it. During this, memory, reflection, anticipation of possible results all come into the process and, like modern computing machines, determine the mode of reaction. In other words, the action is not spontaneous but reactive, or conditioned. Spontaneous action occurs from the physiological level, as when the tendon below the knee is tapped and the foot kicks; or from a slightly higher level as when the hand is withdrawn from a flame; or when instinct of the kind which automatically thinks of a snake as dangerous causes reaction even when more careful observation would show it to be harmless. So that, as the reaction reaches higher levels still and becomes considered and judged, more and more interposes between the sensory stimulus and the reaction. A man receives his bank statement and realises he has very little to his credit. He rarely reacts by snatching cash from a passer-by, he thinks out how to remedy his sad state. Nevertheless, his actions are still reactive and not self-originated. If, moreover, he studies carefully what he wants to do, he will find that, basically, his subsequent acts will be to satisfy what was originally the animal instinct to survive, to be safe, to obtain food and necessities.

So most action is in that sense reactive, and an elaboration of primitive instinctive patterns. But it is also possible for action to initiate from within and independently of any external stimuli, whether immediate or arising more remotely through memory. Such 'pure' action, outgoing and not set to balance incoming stimuli is nevertheless due to impulses coming into the psyche from outside— or deep inside—itself. That is, they enter the psychic field from the deeper levels of man which we have called spirit. Unlike reaction-causing stimuli, coming from the material pole of the psyche, they come from the level of Being, where all things exist only in archetypal form or, to be more exact, lack of form and extension. These stimuli receive their existential form, their extension in space-time, in the realm of the psyche and, through it, become acts in the external world having a truly creative quality. It is from this that works of art arise, and every really new and original thing is done.

Thus the overall picture of the psyche of man is one where the Self is reflected into the psychological ego and becomes the centre of consciousness in the personality. It links the sphere of Being with that of existence in the physical worlds. It also causes a dichotomy to appear as between spirit and matter which the selfless animal would not know (whence the peace of the pre-self-conscious state of the Garden of Eden). Man alone differentiates between good and evil, Nature and God, and for a long evolutionary period sees them as antagonists. There is a tension created between the two poles of his being, which he feels to be respectively Satanic and Divine; and his whole nature becomes imbued with the sense of his being dragged constantly between opposite forces, the one drawing him back into the past, towards his prehuman origins, the other towards his spiritual or divine future. In other words, the psyche is Nietzsche's " rope over an abyss " on which man cannot stand still, go back, or go forwards without peril; though by going forward he reaches a goal where he destroys himself as man as he becomes more than man.

A verse in the cryptic *Stanzas of Dzyan* whose text is known only as given by H. P. Blavatsky is highly apposite. It says,

' Father-Mother spin a Web, whose upper end is fastened to Spirit, the Light of the One Darkness, and the lower one to its shadowy end, Matter, and this is the Web of the Universe, *spun out of the two Substances made in One* '. (My italics).

Man is traditionally held to be a microcosm, a small replica of the greater universe. Hence the body can be taken as the ' shadowy end ' of the web, the spirit as the ' light ', and the psyche itself as the web between: child of both, partaking of the qualities of both, and, until some resolution takes place, in a state of tension between both, with the ego centre in the middle of the conflict. Indeed it may be suggested that without this conflict the ego would not become manifested, established as a centre of growth, and hence the place where the evolutionary process makes itself felt in the human sphere.

5

SURVIVAL AND IMMORTALITY

WE have here again two terms which are often confused. The distinction between them is, however, of profound importance.

Most intelligent people can introspect sufficiently to discover for themselves that time as we usually think of it is something outside of ourselves: a natural sequence of events which would take place whether we were there or not. The sun would rise and set, the tides would flow, the seasons change in an orderly manner were mankind to vanish from the globe. The conscious human being, with his many complicated activities, at some time discovered that it was convenient to him even if it was not absolutely necessary, for him to gear his daily life into this natural order, and so he invented clocks: a means of measuring time and anticipating or looking back on natural events. In this way he could plan his life, arrange to meet others, and so on. But if he studies the matter, he discovers that without some mechanical means of measurement, and if he is cut off from observation of the position of the sun, and so on, his assessment of physical time is apt to be highly erratic. If he is interested in something, an hour is gone very quickly. In boredom it appears as long as half a day. Moreover, it is well established that in sleep, while the body is quiescent, dream time seems to acquire a certain independence from clock time, events piling up on one another in a few seconds whereas they might spread over several months in waking life. There is the often reported case where a man dreamed that water was dripping very slowly from a tap in his bathroom. Between the drips a great deal of dream events took place. But the dripping became faster and faster, that is, less and less of the drama of the dream occurred between the drips, until he finally woke up to find the sound was in reality the absolutely regular ticking of his watch. In other words, the deeper he was asleep, the more rapidly his mind dramatised itself in his dream, and the nearer he was to physical consciousness, the more nearly he was forced into giving physical time value to his dream material.

This suggests that in whatever state we are apart from the physical body, time instead of being rigid acquires a certain plasticity and elasticity. But it is far from being abolished, since there is sequence in the events we experience in our minds. They do not occur simultaneously. So we can already envisage two worlds or levels of existence, governed by two different orders of time: the physical where time is fixed and ' absolute ', which we measure by means of our clocks; and one where it is plastic and elastic. The latter is the level of psychic or mental activity. It should be added that the same principle applies to space measurement. In the physical world, size, distance, etc., are definite and consistent, while in dreams and other mental activities the same plasticity and elasticity is easily seen to be the rule, the shape and size of things changing, distance being of no account.

It is more difficult and rarer to experience yet a third order of being. This is where both space and time are transcended and the individual finds himself in a realm of universality and eternity. This is the place of vision which saints and mystics have tried in vain to describe directly to us. It is also the place in which the indirect expression of true art finds its roots. Many books have been written about and around this state of ' cosmic ' or ' universal ' consciousness. Many people too have experienced it for themselves, perhaps without recognizing it for what it was, in moments of ecstatic contemplation, when deeply touched, whether by beauty, suffering, love, or in a thousand other ways. Without expanding on this, it is clear that man has that in himself which dwells outside the time-space realm, in a condition of eternity which is also coupled with universal extension throughout the whole of space. Rare and precious as is the moment of vision of this world, it is nevertheless usually of greater value than any other and more extended experience. Its impact is such that the one who undergoes it is permanently changed in some way and in some degree. But it shows him something which is at once utterly familiar because it has always been there, yet also utterly new because he has perhaps never seen it consciously before.[1]

To abbreviate the discussion, we learn by this that the threefold division of man into spirit, soul

[1] See The *Timeless Moment* by Warner Allen, *Watcher on the Hills* by Raynor Johnson, *Cosmic Consciousness* by Bucke, etc.

and body, is consistent with three levels of time (and space) experience. At the two poles of the human constitution we have the spirit, living in a world which is timeless and spacially universal; and the body, meshed into natural space-time, with which it has to conform. Between the two is the soul or psyche, in a world which has the qualities of the dense physical insofar as space and time still exist there, but also something of the spiritual, timeless world. The mixture gives space and time in that region a fluidity which the dense physical world has not.

The timeless world is that of Being, that of rigid space-time that of existence in its fullest extension. That between combines something less than pure Being with something less formed and organized in space-time than physical existence.

From all this we can deduce a probable theory about the relative mortality and immortality of the human psyche. For, clearly, the spirit is beyond the cyclic movement of time, while the body is geared into it; hence the former is immortal the latter mortal. The intermediate psyche has something of both attributes, some degree of immortality from the spiritual pole, some degree of mortality derived from the bodily pole. Hence it seems likely that it survives the death of the body yet does not have everlasting life as does the spirit. Yet if certain aspects of the psyche derive from the spiritual level, these would endure and pass from life to life, while other qualities, of a more earthly nature would tend to drop away after a time, leaving behind only traces or, to use the Sanskrit word, 'skandhas', bundles of potentialities of response, the fruits of incarnate experience.

This difference between immortality and survival is seemingly not appreciated in many quarters, yet it is of paramount importance. Not only is immortality of far greater moment than temporal survival, but when we think of Adam Smith and Eve Brown, it makes us wonder what and how much of the personalities we knew by those names goes beyond the grave, and for how long. This matter can only be resolved as we delve below the surface of their outer being and come to understand the factors which determine their fate. Before doing this, however, a digression into some of the means which can help us will be of use.

6

Parapsychology, Psychology and Survival

Parapsychology, the modern term for what used to be called psychical research, is nowadays a recognized branch of scientific psychology. It can be said to have established (in the words of Professor William MacDougal) 'beyond reasonable doubt' the existence of certain powers of the mind which are still called 'paranormal', or 'beyond the normal'. But, increasingly, the idea of abnormality is fading, as more and more people are found to possess these powers in some degree. The omnibus name 'Psi' is applied to the mental faculties which include, on the one hand, a perceptive function which does not depend on the physical organs of sense: extra-sensory perception, or e.s.p., for short; and, on the other, the active power of mind over matter called psychokinesis, or pk. . The first includes telepathy, clairvoyance, precognition or prophecy of the future, and retrocognition, or reading back into the ' memory ' of objects, (this used to be called psychometry), and all the perceptive side of things. The latter, pk., covers physical phenomena in spiritualism, ' magic ' (both of these when genuine, and not merely forms of the conjurers' art), the feats of certain orders of yogis and dervishes, and, by extension, the effect of one mind on another in such a way that the other mind becomes aware of it in telepathy. Even the action of the mind on one's own body is sometimes included in pk. . To such a degree have the findings of parapsychology become acceptable to all unprejudiced scientists who have studied the evidence (and many have not), that it is becoming increasingly merged into the general field of normal psychology. It is less and less being thought of as concerned with abnormalities, though the term persists in practice as denoting a special department of general psychology, much as one can speak of social psychology or physiological or analytical psychology.

This acceptance of the ' paranormal ' has had a twofold result in the matters concerning us in this book. On the one hand it has reopened the age-old idea that there are fields of consciousness and of action beyond the purely physical. This brings back from the limbo of superstition into the world of probable truth an old and universal belief; but the undiscriminating mind is apt to go much further than is warranted. It thinks that, since science accepts so much, it therefore confirms at least in a general way all that mediums and spiritualists claim to be true, including the doctrines of survival of death, and the reality of communication between the physically living and the dead.

In fact, however, the careful investigations of parapsychology, while they open up many possibilities in this line, also raise many doubts. One thing which it establishes more firmly than any other is perhaps the fact of direct and non-verbal communication between mind and mind: telepathy. Moreover, taking its cue from psychology, parapsychology realizes that everything ever known to an individual is somewhere recorded in his memory even if he has forgotten it, and perhaps has never even registered it with this conscious mind. Hence, if a person consults a medium, and asks about a dead relative, he brings with him all his mental material; and the fact that the medium tells him things he has forgotten is no proof that the source on which the medium draws is other than the sitter's own mind. There is no proof that the material comes from the dead person; but nor is there any proof that it is not the mind of the dead person which is the source of the information, if it is true that mind can exist and function apart from a physical brain. Logically, therefore, mediumistic communications might come from either source, and parapsychology neither supports nor denies either possibility: it merely notes the facts observed.

Rarely, however, a medium tells of things quite unknown either to himself, the sitter, or to anybody near. This is more convincing, but even so it does not altogether eliminate telepathy. For this is known at times to operate indirectly, the sitter's mind enabling the medium to relay from there to the mind of the friend on whose behalf the sitter has come. For instance, it might happen that a person goes to a medium to ask about the dead husband of some woman she knows, and receives information which she, the sitter, has never had. But the widow may have this material, and it is possible that the medium, through the sitter's mind, draws on the widow's memories without of necessity the dead man coming into the picture at all as an active factor.

Still more rare are the cases where a medium tells things not known to any living person. There is a classical case where a lost will was found though the existence of it was known only to the man who had drawn it up and then hidden it. The clue to its resting place was given in a series of dreams of the son, which eventually led him to it in a most unlikely manner. Here it is easy and sensible to think that the dead father was anxious for the will to be found. But the very cautious parapsychologist realizes that the proof is by no means absolute because, as Dunne points out in his classical book, *An Experiment with Time*, and others have confirmed, e.s.p. can take the form of looking into the future and seeing events which have not yet taken place in the physical world, but which are going to. It can thus be argued that the dreamer in this case was not of necessity inspired by his father, but was simply looking forward to the time when he would open the family Bible and find the will. It happened that this matter was important and had strong personal and affec- tional attributes, but it nevertheless might be merely of the same order as the more trivial and unimportant precognitions which many people often experience.

These considerations may appear to be mere quibbling. But it is well to appreciate that, while the field of scientific parapsychology does point to the high probability that man has extended perceptive and active powers in the mind, it goes no further than to study these and to try and discover how they operate. And indeed it has found that there are many unexpected twists and quirks in them, producing surprising results. But it does no more than perhaps to speculate as to the actual mechanism involved, or the medium in which thought and feeling is 'transferred', that is, the nature of the psychic worlds themselves. It has no opinion about survival, one way or the other.

If we want to try and study these open questions, the matter has to be approached from a different angle, which, while not strictly scientific, need not therefore be unreasonable—provided it is realized that any and every supposedly factual description of other 'planes' current in theosophical and similar circles is inexact because it is partial and to some extent symbolic rather than factual. These doubts do not in any way imply that those who observe, or claim to observe, the psychic worlds directly, and to explain the mechanisms by which such observation becomes conscious, are inaccurate or incompetent. They arise from the very nature of what is being observed. For, not being ordinary physical phenomena, they function in a way which no language can express exactly. The situation is somewhat like that of a painter projecting a three-dimensional object on to a two-dimensional canvas. His skill in using the tricks of perspective may suggest three-dimensionality and even—as in the case of *trompe-l'oeil*—deceive us until we actually touch the canvas and find that the solid object is not there. In other words, the artist shows us not the object itself, but a partial image, in some ways a symbol, of it. The image is related to the object, reflects something of the reality, but it is not the object itself.

Not only is there this difficulty in the way of describing anything beyond the physical world, but that world itself appears to contain things which have no names. Our language is derived from the physical world and its ' realities ', and so does not provide proper terms from non-physical subtleties. Thus to describe a psychic colour as ' blue ', or even ' dark blue ', or, further, ' luminous dark blue ' is, as many sensitive people know, highly misleading: it is all these things and something more, which eludes verbal expression; so that, apart from the picture-painter's limitations, there is another one which adds further to the inadequacy of the description of that which is discerned.

With this in mind we shall readily see how lightly descriptions of the world in which any after-life is lived have to be taken: as symbolic rather than strictly factual, and with the assurance that, when expressed in factual terms, things are not really but only symbolically so. Thus the cigarette smoked by a dead young man—assuming him to be actually doing anything of the kind in his posthumous state— is probably not a cigarette at all, but something more or less remotely connected with the thing we know by that name in the physical world. Hence we need always to have in the back of our minds the cautionary phrase, that "it is as if . . . . ." to remind us that things are not what they appear to be. To do this is entirely legitimate, for it serves as a pragmatic manner of studying a subject. In science, the chemist often learns a lot from using beads and balls to make up a model of a certain molecule, but he knows all the time that the actual molecule is not like the model, since it consists of whirling vortices and streams of energy and not of bead-like particles on wires.

In the same way we can consider some of the problems of life after death or out of the body, using for that purpose both the data provided from direct psychic observation, or what purport to be such, and also material derived from psychological and other sources of knowledge of the human mind or psyche. This makes room for a further factor which comes into play and which gives the student a non-dogmatic certainty about this or any other matter of importance. It is expressed in a gentle and unemotional, ' I know ', which is a contrast to the forceful, ' I believe ', which is the mark of the person who wants to know but is still uncertain. This factor, the intuition, is what the French call *la conviction intime*, and extends beyond the frontiers of pure reason and logic, and, though non-rational, makes rational things which reason alone cannot. It is only in this way that the seeker can become really satisfied with the answers to his problems. Reason and logic alone do not replace quiet inner conviction, useful as they are on the way.

In brief, therefore, it can be said that science has widened the field beyond that of utter materialism and logical positivism. But what it gives with one hand, it takes away with the other. It opens up for us the consideration of much material and circumstantial evidence (which, of course, is not proof but a pointer towards proof) previously thought unworthy of attention. At the same time it casts doubt on much which the credulous were inclined to accept at face value though that face was false. It also makes room for the non-rational yet highly potent function of an intuitive sense which, when it is properly used, transcends the limitations of the purely rational and satisfies as no mere logic can.

7

The Pattern of Relatedness

A FURTHER digression from our main theme will strengthen the ground for discussion of life after death. It concerns the matter of personal relationships, in which two main aspects can be discerned. One is true relatedness, the other, identification. To distinguish between them is important since the first is free, forward-moving and creative, while identification enslaves.

Psychologists have learned that there can be in the mind a certain procedure which is called projection. It coincides closely with what psychically perceptive people describe when a person is attracted by desire towards another person or an object. Whether one considers such a description as factual in the space-time aspect of the psychic world, or as pure analogy, it seems that attraction results in a kind of tentacle reaching out from the psyche of the individual and twining itself round the desired object, holding it and trying to draw it towards himself. If, then, some part of the thought-feeling of the individual, as it were, flows down the tentacle and becomes involved in the attachment to the object, a further step takes place, which is *identification* of the personal ego-centre with the object or person. Objectivity, which is the power to examine a thing from outside, is lost and the two people, or the individual person and the object, become interlocked and so in some measure interdependent.

This is easily understood when desire is positive and attractive. It is perhaps not so clear when it is in the form of aversion, yet it operates in just the same manner. The ' tentacle ' would then represent an attempt, not to draw in but to repel, to fend off the thing or person disliked. And, here too, some part of the psyche of the individual may become entangled in the situation. The part projected would then be of some feared or rejected aspect of oneself. That is why one who, let us say, rejects his own sexual nature, automatically reacts against anything which is kin to that side of himself, and so leads him to what is often a confused and exaggerated horror of that aspect of natural life. Moreover, his fears may make him see danger where no danger exists. Most people dislike snakes and shy away from them when they meet them even when they are harmless. But if, in the dusk, they project their fear of snakes onto a piece of stick in the path, that stick to all intents and purposes *becomes* a snake for the moment, and the reaction is just as it would be towards a real one.

Projection from the mind can also occur without external objects. A person who constantly thinks of a certain person or situation develops in his psyche a tendency to repeat the thought time after time. This creates a mental habit which may become automatic, and gradually the ego loses control of it. It can then become a more or less autonomous ' thought form ' or ' complex ' in the person's mind, sometimes visible to a clairvoyant almost as if it were a separate entity. It is created by the mind-force known in Sanskrit as *Kriyashakti*, or the creative energy of the mind, the word usually taken to be mind working at its own level, but also used in much the same way as the parapsychologist's conception of psycho-kinesis, as the power of mind over matter.

Such a thought-form may be of any quality from the most elevated to the most debased. It may be that the individual, through fear of his own instinctive nature and its passions, creates his own devils and believes himself to be possessed or obsessed by external entities. But it can equally be that the image is of a Master or Saviour, a God or some kind of high spiritual Being. Naturally, too, the thought-form has something of the quality that the creator puts into it; and it cannot be denied that it may also tend to attract some of the ' material ', or energies which have the same ' wavelengths ', in the collective mind, which encourage the individual to think that these are indeed entities—of whatever order—independent of himself. But they are in reality actually part of himself. He often, indeed usually, fails to recognize himself as the creator of his own gods or devils, and so poses a serious problem to psychiatrists if not to his friends.

Relatedness is, however, something quite different. It means that an individual finds himself responding to another person without wanting or expecting anything of him or her. He feels a harmony, a complementariness in the other person, so that while each remains emotionally quite free of the other, there is yet a happy, creative and loving field between them. It is true to say that in a true and perfect relationship there is a very full awareness of that other person and even of faults which one dislikes; yet the whole person is accepted, faults and all, without adverse reaction or rejection. Relatedness is based on love: the kind of love which the saint has for his fellow men, feeling neither superior nor inferior, but *akin*. Martin Buber expresses it and the sense of respect involved when he speaks of an ' I-Thou ' relationship as distinct from that of ' I-Him/Her/It '; the latter implying in some way a barrier between the two.

In actual fact, every human relationship is almost certain to be a compound of both things, relatedness and identification. To be entirely objective and unpossessive, or unrejecting of the whole of an intimate such as husband, wife, child or parent, (these especially because of the common blood or germ-plasm ties) is beyond mere human capacity; which is why we have to be prepared to admit to ourselves that, however philosophical and objective we may be, the acts in life, or the death of another, will hurt us. The best we can do is to realize that free relatedness is the thing to be cultivated, both for the sake of ourselves and of the other person, so that identification is reduced to a minimum. This makes for both health and happiness at all times. It can only be achieved by the growth of self-awareness which, by showing how and what we project into our daily relationships, enables us to cease from identifying with others at the instinctive levels too and shift our focus of consciousness to the higher reaches of feeling and thinking, and hence towards the more spiritually illumined levels of the psyche.

8

Death and After

All the discussion in earlier chapters has been intended to lead up to the problem of what happens when man dies or, at any rate, soon after. No *proof* or solution can be offered and, indeed, science knows that it is unlikely ever to have even direct *evidence* that man continues, when he leaves his body, in any personal form. At best the evidence is indirect and circumstantial; though there is, even after discarding much that is dubious, a considerable amount of material which points towards this probability. On the other hand, if we take into account what we know of man, both from occultism and psychology, couple this with certain recorded experiences, give due weight to traditions and beliefs, however distorted these may have become, and add to this the material provided by

certain people who claim to be able to observe the
after-world and its denizens directly by means
of e.s.p., we can build up a certain hypothesis
which is consistent in itself. In this all these
contributing factors are included and play their
part. It is, moreover, surprising how well they
fit together, except for the more emotional accounts
given by spiritualism, in which wishful thinking
plays so large a part that it cannot be taken too
seriously. (Who has ever heard of a communication supposedly from the dead to be otherwise than
affectionate, or saying that life 'in spirit' is
anything but sentimentally happy and gay? Yet is
there any reason why this should be so? As we shall
see, there is on the contrary good ground for
thinking things may not always be as rosy as this,
truth being often unpalatable when it has to be
starkly faced.)

There is also something to be gained from some
works of 'fiction'. I use this word in quotations
because what we call fiction is not of necessity what
the rigid puritan would call lies or fantasy. On
the contrary, it represents reality of another order
from that of the external physical world, an inner
psychic reality of the author's own. And when
it comes to such works as L.A.G. Strong's *Corporal*

Tune, Evelyn Underhill's *The Grey World*, Arnold Bennett's *The Dream* or Monica Redlich's *The Various Light*, it becomes clear that the writer has here built into a story a considerable amount of personal experience of another order of life from that of the plain physical. They present it in a sober, unsentimentalized form in which the 'fiction' belongs only to the characters and details of the stories themselves, not to the background of other-wordliness against which they play. Even Algernon Blackwood's charming, if rather fanciful, tales often have a ring of something familiar and real, while many poets also speak of the world beyond this one as if they were on familiar ground. So they too can be taken into account if used with discrimination.

We shall come to the actual experience of physical death later on, and will discuss it as best we can. But let us now think of what is reasonably likely when the body has been shed, if that is not the end of the individual life. What appears probable is that, after whatever intermediate stages there may be, the individual becomes conscious at the psychic level: that where he is no longer incarnate in the flesh, but where he is no more and no less 'in spirit', (to use the spiritualist's phrase, but meaning by spirit what is discussed in chapter 3.) than he was in physical life. He is, mentally, much what he was in physical life.

If the mind is, as psychologists believe, an organized field of psychic energies in which the personal ego or self dwells, this idea seems logical. Moreover, there are endless tales where somebody, extremely ill, anaesthetised, unconscious as a result of accident, finds himself able to look at his body in bed or on the ground, to note the surroundings, to be conscious of what is being said, and all the time to feel himself as ' I ', able to think, feel, remember, perceive, in much the same way as under normal conditions. It is only the dense body which is out of the picture. On their ' return ' to what one at least referred to as a much diminished state of consciousness in a very sick body, they have at times been able to recall their out-of-the-body experience and to record it. One even went so far as to say, ' I know now what death is '. From the evidential viewpoint these accounts are telling, though it must be admitted that the flaw is that the person did not actually die and pass on. How much this helped or conditioned their memory it is hard to say, but on the whole the material suggests that when a person is .o all intents and purposes dislocated from his body nd brain, he is still himself, ' in psyche ', and able to carry on normal psychic functions.

Indeed, there is a comparison between the state of the disembodied person in such a case and the ordinary dreamer who is still ' I ', still thinks and feels; but he does not consciously observe his body as something apart from himself. It is as if the dislocation of the psyche in physiological sleep consisted largely in closing certain channels of sensory perception so that the dreamer is in-turned and dealing, as a rule, with subjective material in the psyche, while physical trauma, drugs and the like sometimes do not shut observation of the physical world out of the field of the conscious mind.

This inward turning of the dreamer while he is unconcerned with his body is in keeping with the tradition in, for instance, the Tibetan *Book of the Dead* which speaks of a period of ' swoon ' following loss of the body. Many descriptions of the after-life given by non-mediumistic clairvoyants echo this, notably C. W. Leadbeater, giving it as their own observation (though here it has to be allowed that the observers may have been influenced by what they had read).

If this unconscious ' swoon '—which in reality may well be one of very complete yet active introversion as a reaction from the enforced extraversion of physical life—is the general rule, there seem to be cases where it is either very brief or else comes after a time when loose ends of physical life are straightened out. There is for instance the case of a very wise and enlightened man who died serenely in bed and who found means of communicating through a clairvoyant friend within a few hours of his physical death. She suddenly became aware of him, saying briefly and tersely, ' Tell my wife that a certain paper in my wallet is important. She may not realise it ', then vanished. The message, passed on, came soon after the wife had found the paper and did not know whether or not it should be kept. There is also the famous Chaffin case, where it took some weeks before the dead man's will was found, as a result of a series of dreams by his son. Here nobody but the dead man knew of the existence of that will nor where it would be found. When this was all settled, there is no published record of any further dream or other contact with the father.

Both these instances suggest that the dead person apparently showed concern for those dear to him.

So does the case recorded in my wife's and my book, *The Psychic Sense*, (2nd ed., p. 62) where an airman killed in a crash was much worried over his wife's financial future, and managed to find a person through whom to communicate; and, here, he seemed to know in advance that the communicator would be called in to see his wife in a state of shock and collapse, though this was only arranged some days after his ' talk ' with the clairvoyant.

All similar instances point in the direction of survival and, in these cases, of clear awareness of at least some physical things. In the interests of truth, however, it should be added that though this is the simple and obvious explanation, it still does not *prove* anything absolutely. We know enough of the phenomena of precognition, as well as of the dramatic power of the mind, to realize that a combination of these could be the real answer. But both precognition and dramatization are such constant occurrences (see Dunne's *Experiment with Time*) that one has also to ask oneself why they should operate in this particular way at this particular time of crisis in the lives of people who were not the direct recipients of the messages.

There is, moreover, something in common between these experiences and the tradition of the restless ghost who cannot free himself from an earth-bound state until certain problems have been resolved or sins expiated. It is as if ties of an emotional nature were able to influence to some extent and, at least for a while, the stages of the posthumous life: a subject on which there will be more to say.

There is another interesting possible clue which, as we shall see, also fits in with tradition. It arises from an instance where a certain person interested in parapsychology had a dream about Sir Oliver Lodge, whom she had met a number of times. In the dream, Lodge was speaking to her and explained that after death memory of details and incidents in physical life tended to fade, and only principles remained. There seemed no particular reason for the dream except that at the time the dreamer was engaged in writing about such matters as survival and its nature. Next morning the mail brought the Journal and other papers of the Society for Psychical Research, which reported on the frustration of certain experiments which had been conducted for years. These had been planned by several well-known people, including

Lodge, prior to their deaths. They had written on a slip of paper a few lines relating some trivial incident in their lives. This paper had been enclosed in a series of envelopes on which were written clues more and more generalised, about this incident. Instructions were left that the writers would try and communicate personally through mediums, and that when the survivors— a competent set of parapsychologists—felt they had some reason to think the communication genuine, they should open one envelope after another, and so get closer to the mysterious enclosure. They had now got to one envelope where Lodge had stated, ' Do not open this unless you are sure that it is I who am communicating '; and, try as they would, they felt they could not satisfy the condition. The papers from the Society were already in the mail when the dream occurred, and there may have been some precognition in the case. The principal issue, however, was that Lodge, if it was he, was explaining why the experiment could not now be completed: he had been ' dead ' too long and could not remember what was on the original slip of paper.

Taking all the material available, it suggests that, speaking in the language of clock time, when the body is lost, the clear focus of physical life and its details tends to become blurred, leaving in the mind a kind of quintessence of experience, the principles of things and not their minutiae.

Once again we have some comparison between the after-death state and the dream life, where it is known that the more deeply asleep the individual, the more he seems remote from the rigidity with which the body and its consciousness are meshed into clock time. There are many dreams which show this and how it is really as the dreamer begins to wake that he finds himself gradually more engaged in time. During sleep he is, seemingly, less tied in with exactitude and precision as we know them in physical life.

Indeed, if we study dreams sufficiently they suggest to us a great deal which may be objectively true about the conditions we may expect to meet when we have left our body for good. True, dreams are usually symbolic or dramatized versions of the contents of our own minds, but the nature of the pictures can be taken as in some way related to the world in which they take place: a plastic, flexible, yet ordered world, with its depths and its heights—taking these words as referring to qualities and not in a spatial sense. Some dreams reflect bodily states even so trivial as indigestion; some bring in physical sounds such as the ticking of a clock or the sound of a bell; while, through endless gradations of quality, and hence of psychological impact and significance, they reach a level where the images into which we translate them have transcendental, spiritual value. The latter are where gods, saviours, angels, heroes and other symbols of spiritual archetypes appear. It is, incidentally, rare rather than common, as is sometimes suggested, that a dream is a straight ' astral experience ' or memory of objective events in the psychic world, or seen from that level while they occur at the physical level. How much of objective psychic experience becomes woven into a dream is a thing difficult to determine but, in any case, it is almost always adapted to the subjective meaning of that dream and the inner personal problem it represents.

It seems probable therefore that when a person physically dies, he will find himself in a state already familiar since he is in it during sleep. The only abrupt change will be that he has no longer a physical anchorage to which to return. The presence of that anchorage may in some measure help him during physical life to steady, focus and balance his psychic activity, and its total absence after death may be a cause of temporary bewilderment. This is brought out by the account of a man who awoke one morning with the sense that his body acted somewhat like the weight on a pendulum, slowing down activity, or the governor on an engine which keeps it at a constant speed. He felt that if this were detached, his mind might race off at top speed, almost out of control because, having no relatively slow-moving brain through which to work, everything would go ' with the speed of thought ' and without his having time to consider and look around him. If he thought of China, he would, as he put it, find himself there without knowing how he got there, and if his next thought was of the South Pole, again he would be whisked off in a flash.

This fanciful description may well have truth in it because there is at death a clear and well marked break in the totality of the field in which man has lived during incarnation. The heavy, massive physical organism falls away at a certain definite moment of time, but the rest of the field and the background or medium in which that field exists seems to be the same. And, as in dreams, it is not a series of broken steps reaching from the

The Mirror of Life and Death

physical to the spiritual through separate ' planes '
—etheric, astral, mental—but a continuum. In
much the same way, the waters of the ocean deeps,
dense and compressed, are continuous from the
ground below them to the surface, where they are
under less pressure, and where the light of the
sun penetrates.

If this is so, one may expect progression after
the death of the body to be, not a series of further
deaths as the subtler ' bodies ' are sloughed off
one by one, but a much more unified movement
of consciousness from the level of contact with the
physical world towards some other level which
may be compared, as far as the psyche is concerned,
with the surface where the sea meets with the air:
air standing for spirit, and no longer the psychic
or soul-levels of life. It may be added that, though
this is beyond our ken, there may at this level be
no such division as there is between the bottom of
the sea—the physical world—and the water, or
between the surface of that water and atmosphere.
There may, rather, be a continuous movement
comparable to that of a ship at sea when it moves
across the equator from one hemisphere into the
other: spirit, though ' external ' to psyche, is
within the human field, as the chemical and dense

96

physical is not (see our booklet *Man Incarnate*, as also descriptions of man as *five*-fold).

If, then, the sphere in which the after-life begins and for some time endures, is such a continuum; and if the dead person enters this sphere free from the need for daily return to physical occupations, we can speculate further on the stages he may go through.

For one thing, his mind or psyche will be as it was, active or petrified, harmonious or in conflict. The *libido*, to use the somewhat unfortunate term applied to psychic energy in depth psychology, which is the life-force or *prana* of the psyche, will still be there as it was in life. This energy causes attraction or repulsion towards objects, people and events, and its habits would persist. But there would be the difference, that it no longer had the necessary mechanism to operate in the physical world, and hence to reach out to the objects of physical sense which in some measure are the goal of the ordinary human being. Some are more attached to them than others, some have, as they aged in their bodies, realized their comparatively small value even in terms of pleasure —or its opposite. In any case, these objects are now out of reach. At best the creative,

image-making faculty of the psyche may create simu-
lacra, similar, but non-physical, and " imaginary "
objects, out of its own activity. We do this in
ordinary dreams, but dream objects seem then to
have an elusive quality, to fade away or change
just as we are ready to grasp them, and as our
minds move as regards them. One can thus
conceive of the craving for physical things and
pleasures resulting only in disappointment and
frustration. This can only end as the individual,
beginning to know himself as no longer physically
alive, withdraws his energies from a futile quest.

Another factor in the posthumous situation also
derives from the state of mind of the deceased.
During life, one of the functions of the brain is to
allow concealment of underlying motives and
feelings. One is conscious only of just so much at
a time, while alive and awake; but psychiatrists
have discovered beyond any question that besides
the conscious motive for many things in life there
are other, unconscious layers of the mind which
we may not care to acknowledge. These often
have more power in determining conscious action
and conscious mental attitudes than reason, logic,
and actual physical events. It is also known that
in sleep, or when a person is hypnotized or

half-drugged, the field of awareness widens: total concealment is no longer possible, and the conflicting elements within ourselves tend to come within the reach of conscious knowledge. After death the screen is no longer there, and it seems probable that we have to come face to face with our true feelings, thoughts, attitudes to things and people, without being able any longer to evade them. The ' pure ' person may have to face deep sensuality; the superficial ' server ' and altruist may have to see his underlying vanity, self-seeking, pride; the devotee of humane causes, to face his repressed cruelty and hate; the ' pacifist ' his suppressed aggressiveness.

All this builds up into a picture which explains the ordinary doctrine of purgatory through which even orthodoxy realizes that the average man has to pass before he can enter heaven. It is a state of the working-out of the psychic energies directed towards physical pleasures no longer attainable, and also the ordeal of facing the unpleasant truth about oneself.

The force of desire can thus be thought of both as simple and directed towards unattainable physical objects; or it can be thought of as a stream of energies split within itself and causing stress because the different branches are directed towards incompatible ends, the incompatibility being due to a direct antithesis between conscious and unconscious motives. In any person there is probably something of both of these factors, perhaps even in the same complex: desire for some physical pleasure (or the avoidance of pain, which is the same in reverse) and emotional conflict about the same thing. A person may for instance be attracted sexually, or feel the urge to drink alcohol, while he feels at the same time inwardly guilty, because his desire is incompatible with his ideals. During life he hides one side of the situation and relegates it to the unconscious, now he has to face it in its entirety.

Psychic energies, however, follow much the same laws as govern physical energies such as heat or electricity. That is, they are measurable and finite in quantity, they can expend themselves, and they can also neutralize one another so that they cancel out. Unlike physical energies, however, they can be directly controlled by the will of the individual, working through his mind; that is, by the power of choice. It is well known in psycho-therapy that when once both sides of a mental conflict are fully exposed to consciousness, the

individual can then choose—and if he is suffering
pain, fear, stress, usually does choose—what to
do: whether or not to continue to act, think and
feel as he did before, or to embark on a new phase
of life. It is probably the same in the after-death
state. When the individual realizes the futility of
trying to satisfy physical desires, he will gradually
turn away from them; and as he sees the dualities
in himself which cause stress and suffering, he will
gradually find himself in a position to liquidate
the contradictions, so that the opposite pulls cancel
out and he becomes free. In this way purgatory
differs from hell, in that it is a passing phase, not
a permanent one.

Hell is no mere figment, it is something very real.
Unlike the crude ideas of the churches, however, it
can be experienced as much in physical life as
after death. Apart from any wider description of
it, it can be understood simply as the state of mind
of the person who obstinately refuses to see things,
and himself, as they really are. He looks at one
side only and thereby ties himself down ' forever '
—which means, for as long as he does not change
his attitude from within. In other words, hell is a
self-created state; and, as such, freedom can begin
whenever the individual chooses, and allows himself

to pass on into still unpleasant but at least forward-moving state we have called purgatorial.

It should be realized, moreover, that there is no idea in either purgatory or hell of a vindictive, punitive deity condemning the individual to suffer. Natural law, which operates in the psychic as much as in the physical worlds, causes the individual who is ignorant or rebellious against what he knows is right for himself, to bring trouble on himself by his own acts. If then he changes, he sets new forces to work which set him free by his own efforts. This points the moral which is to be found in every kind of spiritual and religious teaching, that self-awareness and self-understanding are of paramount importance to the individual. It is only when such teaching is debased that blind faith, emotional dedication, ' putting one's burdens on Christ ' or the idea of a mechanical absolution from a priest become a substitute for self-help or self-' salvation ' through the dispelling of ignorance both about oneself and about the world one lives in.

For the time being I shall avoid any discussion of the problem of subjectivity and objectivity in after-death experience. What is important is to try and get a general view of the experience of the ' dead ' person, basing this on what information we have. If we remember that the mind can create forms and images out of its own inwardness, but that this mind also dwells in a collective sea of its own kind of material or energies; and if we remember that the forms created by the mind can be so projected that they become detached from the ' I ' and behave as if they existed in their own right, that is all that matters.

On the other hand, it is possible to suggest a mechanical theory of the probable progression of the psyche from its immediate after-death state towards further stages in its journey through time. We can do this in two ways. In one we think of the psyche as material, and hence as having some kind of weight or density. In the other we think of it dynamically as a field of energies directed towards certain ends and purposes. Both are equally valid, and both suggest a certain useful picture.

In terms of matter, we may consider the more earthy aspects of man as denser, more weighty than the subtler and more abstract. They follow the general rule, which is that even in the psychic, non-physical realm, they have some at least of the characteristics of the bodily end of man. Being denser, they tend to find their level near the physical world, just as a heavy body tends to sink towards the floor of the sea, while others of lesser specific gravity float in the middle or upper levels.

In other, more dynamic though still physical language, we can think of the field of the psyche as being animated by forces and energies which draw the ego towards certain things. Just as the magnetism in a compass needle tends to align that needle with the lines of magnetic force between the earth's poles, so does it seem to happen in the psyche. Moreover, as in the case of free magnets, these poles tend to be actively drawn, to move towards, the object of attraction. So if a man, alive or dead, is much attracted towards either the material or spiritual poles of his being, his ego and his conscious field will tend to be drawn towards that pole which is the most powerful. Hence if his passional desires are very strong, he will try and move towards the objects of those desires. It is only as he detaches himself, ceases to keep those desires active (which happens much as an electro-magnet is kept active only by the flow of current in the coil) that he will lose interest and so become free to move elsewhere. So we may take it that a man's psyche ties itself down *from within* to objects of the senses, or to psychic images, or to spiritual ideas, and that it can only free itself as the forces and the energies which cause that tying-in cease to operate, or operate in a different direction.

Clearly, too, the dual pull as between the body and the spirit is felt at its maximum during incarnation. After the body is left behind, it is as if a spring (or, to use the analogy previously used, a web) stretched between two extremes, were let loose at one end—in this case, the ' lower ' or material end. But the loosening is only partial because the forces of desire still oppose the pull from the spiritual end. The ' I ' is not free from its earthly attachments despite the change which has taken place through physical death, so long as he goes on *desiring*. Hence the element of suffering, more or less intense, in the purgatorial conception. But as the ' downward ' or regressive forces weaken, so does the conflict between the two poles. Hence, step by step, one can envisage the psyche passing from a state of stress and pain towards one where this gets less and less, until eventually it ceases altogether. In other words, purgatory is succeeded by heaven.

This is in line with many versions of the same tradition. It is also consistent with what we see happening during physical life, when an individual changes his attitude from one of passionate desire, violent emotional attitudes and the other things which usually bring him into conflict both with himself and those around him. As he alters so does he become happier and more serene. After death the process continues or, if it has not already started, begins.

A further point suggests itself, which is in line with the dream about Lodge. It is that thinking about physical objects with their clear-cut outlines is very concrete and detailed. As thought 'rises', it becomes more abstract and general, concerned with principles and not with contrast between opposites. The best thinker tends more and more towards 'both and', in place of 'either or', because he sees both sides of a question and so tends to integrate them into a larger synthesis. In the same way feeling becomes less, 'for' or 'against', and acquires depth and a sense of true values, bringing with it a quietness which is in marked contrast with the 'emotion' or 'moving out' of the more instinctive, passional end of its range. It seems reasonable to think that this would be the tendency after death, as the individual liquidates the stressful elements which keep him in purgatory and he moves gradually on into a quieter and happier region of the psychic world.

Such an idea is more logical than that which suggests a series of 'deaths': the shedding first of the physical body, then of the 'astral' body of feeling, and so on. True, mental development seems to go in steps rather than a continuous slope, but thought and feeling always go hand in hand in these 'gestalts', parallel with one another at every level. It does not make sense that one should shed the 'feeling body' and go on in a feeling-less 'thought body'. Experience proves that it is not so in physical life, and there is no reason to believe that things change completely when the body is removed. Moreover, how can a person experience the feeling of happiness or bliss always associated with the 'heaven' stage of the after-life if he has left behind the very vehicle by means of which alone the 'I' is capable of feeling? Rather is it reasonable to see thought and feeling ranging continuously and side by side throughout the whole field of the psyche, from its material to its spiritual pole. At the latter end it would be—as those know who have had 'peak experiences'— intense and happy or ecstatic feeling but with none of the sense of 'movement' which accompanies feeling (technically, *affect*) at its more earthly, passional levels. Hence the 'bliss' of heaven.

9

THE MOMENT OF DEATH. JUDGMENT

BEFORE going further and speculating—for it can
be little more—on the later stages of the after-life,
it will be useful to go back and consider the actual
passage from physical life into that where the
psychic life continues without bodily attachment.

It is important to bear always in mind that the
psychic levels of life are always with us, a background to whatever we are doing or experiencing
in the physical body. During the day they become
obscured by the demands of action and sensation
at the physical level but they are nevertheless
constantly at work, balancing any exaggerated
tendency to feel too strongly or wrongly about
the physical realm. Indeed, it has been said that
we dream just as much during waking as during
sleeping time, the only difference being that while

we are awake we are not aware of the dream process; or, to be more exact, less aware of it, since our daydreams lurk on the fringe of consciousness much of the time. The only basic change in this level of life at death is the removal of one of the ' organs ' through which the spiritual Self expresses itself, while using the psyche as an intermediary between itself and the body.

In daily life, at moments of crisis, it is usual for the person with any kind of insight to find that, in one way or another, some new kind of powers, or a sense of inner direction, come into play. It is as if during the time of stress, consciousness rose to a peak where both ability and understanding were increased beyond normal. Physical death is likely to be such a moment of crisis, of movement from one phase of existence into another. It is the end of a time-cycle during which the total man is extended into the world of existence to the maximum extent. At the end of the half-cycle represented by incarnation, it is only to be expected that the dying person may find himself becoming aware of things normally closed to him: all the more so perhaps because his energies, no longer outgoing into action, are inward-turned and hence emphasise the perceptive phase.

This is often the case. Dying people frequently become serene, composed, happy, especially if their death has been gradually led up to through age or illness. If they can speak they may tell of feeling once again in the presence of loved ones who have predeceased them; and they may go further and say that God, or Jesus, or a patron saint, or some other great Being is with them, ministering to their inner welfare and making them feel safe.

Frequently, what they perceive is confused between human and superhuman or non-human elements, but it is possible to analyze their visions into two different classes.

To feel that one is once more in touch with people one loves is a level of experience which belongs to the personality or psyche rather than to spirit. It would be unwise to attempt to dogmatize as to the ' reality ' of that contact. In any case, as we shall discuss later, the question of subjectivity and objectivity, though interesting, is yet in a way unimportant in this connection. What matters at this point is that the individual feels his closeness to the dead. On theoretical grounds it may be argued that they are merely perceiving their own thoughts about them; or else that they are simply becoming aware of a personal contact which had never ceased with the individuals themselves, but of which they were normally as unconscious as they were of dreams while active and awake in physical life. Either of these, or a compound of both, seems more probable than the idea sometimes put forward that the dead relatives gather together in the sick-room and wait as they might wait for the arrival of a friend by train or ship. In any case, the impact on the percipient is personal and comforting.

The other order of vision is theoretically different, and derives from a level of being beyond that of the personal psyche. Gods, saints, angels, are archetypal figures. Their ' dwelling place ' is the spiritual world and they make themselves known and felt in the psyche through dreams and visions which have a quality of potency and show them to be more than the usual run of imaginative pictures. Whether they emerge from within the individual or whether they arise from ' outside ', coming out from their own world to help him, is irrelevant when one realizes that in the spiritual world there is no ' I ' and ' Not-I ', and that all is not merely united but actually and factually One. The images, however, do come from

' outside ' insofar as they enter the field of the mind from beyond the limits of the actual psyche.

The exact form in which a universal archetype is perceived is, however, personal, and is determined by the thinking-feeling habits of the individual mind. Thus a Christian may perceive a certain archetype as Jesus, a Buddhist as Gotama Buddha, another as the Master to whom he has given his devotion, and so on. This in no way denies the independent existence of spiritual Beings such as we have named, or of angels and other non-human entities. But the thing which makes them what they are and gives them their potency in the psychic world is the spiritual, numinous quality which is theirs. It is as if the *numinous*, spiritual archetypal Essence of them took on *phenomenal* form according to the mental habit of the one to whom they become evident. In this way it can be said that the dying person has become more consciously open to his own spiritual nature, receiving from it a sense of support and strength, of companionship in what would otherwise seems to be the great loneliness of death.

It should be noted also that there is everywhere a tradition that there are agencies, often described as angelic or devic, which attend man at times like birth, severe illness or death. In Jewish and Muslim lore, the Angel of Death is called Azrael. Experience confirms the tradition, as it also does the fluidity of the form in which such agencies are perceived.

Whether sudden and unexpected death contains a period of inner vision of this kind it is hard to say, for those who have been on the brink of death and returned to life can, obviously, tell only part of the story. Drowning people frequently speak of having had a moment of recollection in which the whole of their past life stood before them in minutest detail and absolute clarity. Whether this is the case at every death one cannot say. But old people tend to go back to their past life, to live over again their early years, to bring up memories and events which they seemed long since to have forgotten. Perhaps the complete picture only appears in concentrated form at the very moment they die.

One thing however is not clear from the accounts we have, which is how far back the vision extends. None speak of going back beyond birth, yet it is well known that the unborn child has some kind of consciousness in the womb and possibly if we had the whole picture, we should find that the vision embraced not merely the span of the past incarnation but could be carried back through time to the very emergence of the individual from the mass consciousness of prehuman life. It is unwise to speculate too much on this matter, but it might well be that the extent of the experience would depend on the degree to which the personal mind was infused with timeless, spiritual insight, hence with that aspect of it which is continuous from beginning to end of its path through humanity.

This aspect of things has to do with the past. It is reflected in myth in the universal belief in there being some kind of Judgment immediately after death. In Egypt this is dealt with extensively, where the soul is shown as weighed in the scales before an assembly of officiating divine figures before being relegated to is proper sphere. In Tibet there is a similar story where the soul is equated with a bouncing ball, oscillating between a high and a low point before finding its true place. These legends also agree with the ideas in the last chapter which suggest a mechanical analogy in which the discarnate psyche finds its level according to its psychic specific gravity, moving to other levels as that specific gravity changes.

The whole concept coincides with the idea, not of a punitive, vindictive trial before an external god, but with a process of finding a true balance of psychic forces out of the totality the individual ' brings with him ' into the after-death realm which is now his home. He brings with him a quantity of material, unsorted, confused, contradictory, and this bundle now has to be tied up and harmonized before he can go further. The presiding judge at this assize is none other than his spiritual Self, working within the framework of ineluctable and universal law.

Thus far we have considered matters arising out of the past of the individual. Each one, however, has also a future: a goal, a teleology, a *dharma*, in which his individual uniqueness reaches its fruition. It is perhaps for obvious reasons that the one who has been on the brink of death does not report anything about vision of this future: he has not gone through the critical point which may have to be passed before it is perceived as a sequence leading on from the immediate present. The old man or woman, however, traditionally ' dreams dreams ' as well as delving into the past, and we know from depth psychology that dreams often, if not always, contain a teleological element. They tell us where we are and what the immediate problem is, and also what is the clue to resolution of that problem so that we can move forward.

Lacking reports of the total experience of the dying man, we can nevertheless derive something from both tradition and the fact that the old ' dreamer of dreams ' is already looking forward in evolution. It seems logical that just as the past becomes focused into a given moment, as in the case of the nearly-drowned, thereby completing the backward-looking of the old in a flash of intensity, so may the future, represented in the latent potentialities as yet not actualized in each one of us. If, then, there comes an instant where past and future, actual and potential, meet, the individual would obtain a vision of the whole of himself, spirit, soul and body, past experience and future unfoldment, in one synthetic and transcendental moment of insight. He would see himself in his totality, from the point of view of that in him which IS; and at the same time he would, from the angle of himself as a time-existing ego, be face to face with the ISNESS in himself: his God, his true Self, or whatever name he may care to give it.

There is of course no proof of this, but ancient lore insists, in one form or another, that this instant of complete insight (which is another term for what is called judgment) is also that at which the individual has an opportunity to move right out of the sphere of time and rebirth and to enter a new state where Being takes the place of existence, eternity replaces time, and in practical terms, the personal time-ego merges into the real Self.

There will be more to say about such a transition; but for the dying person it means that there is an instant when, if he is attentive and ready, he can, to use Buddhist language, leave the wheel of time and rebirth and enter Nirvana: not by going through stage after stage on the time-track, but by moving off in another dimension from that of time, and entering eternity. He then becomes what in the east is termed an *Arhat*, or ' enlightened man ', free from any obligation to be reborn, yet also free to choose so to be if it serves his purposes.

If he uses the opportunity provided by this passing moment, he has, in a sense, no after-life: he is free from the stages which we have adumbrated and is henceforth in command of his own destiny. In Indian terms he will have found *moksha*, in Christian terms, he will have become one of ' God's saints ' and entered heaven. The potentiality of this occurring is there—as indeed it is with us all the time—but most people miss the moment and it is gone as they move past it to remain still in the realm of time and causality, tied down by their own inattention, or ignorance, or their desires for time-objects. So they have to go round the cycle once more, and then again, until they are ready to move off into the eternal. Hence the Christian hope that the ordinary man becomes beatified and sanctified when he loses his body, and without having already prepared the way deeply within himself, seems unduly optimistic where the great majority are concerned. But it is not impossible, it seems, that such a thing can in principle happen.

It is because of the belief that physical death offers a particular opportunity to the departing soul that all the rites and prayers for the dying exist. In Tibet the officiant catechises the dying and even the dead man at length, telling him what he may expect, and also of the thing for him to try and achieve. In other countries matters are usually less explicit, but the ceremonies and customs are all aimed at helping the individual to make the best of what happens to him as he dies. Many of these rites are debased, and travesties of what might be done, but it cannot be denied that, if only telepathically, thoughts of goodwill, affection and hope may indeed be of real value to the one who is entering a new phase of existence at the moment of physical death

As a footnote to this chapter, since it deals with the matter of the Judgment it is apposite to add a few words about the belief in lost souls, which exists everywhere in the world. These are said to be the relics of people who have failed to make the grade into progressive experience, to enter heaven or even purgatory, and are therefore doomed to extinction.

Once more, in line with Kant, such a belief cannot be summarily dismissed, especially when we think of what appears to be the vast wastage all round us in the universe. Stars break up, so do planets within stellar systems; and, nearer home, we see species dying out or never maturing, millions of spermatozoa never fertilizing an ovum, and many other examples of what seems to be frustrated evolution. Is there, one has to ask oneself, any reason why germinal human individuals should not also undergo wastage? In Blavatskian philosophy such a thing is taken for granted as part of the universal law, though it is not thought of in the same way as the fundamentalist Christian or Moslem as the fate of every unbeliever. It is understood that the evolutionary stream would normally carry the ordinary human being with it towards ' salvation ', *moksha*, liberation, *nirvana*, whether or not he does much about it. Not to reach this point at some time, perhaps aeons hence, would require much hard work on the part of the individual. But the possibility remains that if a man chooses to misuse his freewill he may by, so to speak, constantly rowing upstream against the evolutionary tide, succeed in destroying himself for good. As we know, it is much harder work to move against the tides than to float idly with them, hence it is safe to assume that it is much more difficult to become a ' damned ' soul than to be ' saved '. Few, if any, would have the will, the courage, the endurance, as well as the complete dedication to what is considered evil, to stay the course until the amputation of the personal soul from the spiritual Self had reached a point of no return.

10

Heaven

We have so far discussed two traditional after-death states. There remains a third, that of heaven or paradise. As usual, this popular belief needs careful scrutiny and, as so often, clarification comes from the East and is all the more valuable and practical in that it coincides with the idea of man as basically spirit, incarnating in a relatively temporal psyche and a wholly temporal body.

In India two kinds of heaven are distinguished. One is called *Moksha* or *Nirvana*, final liberation and union with the Absolute, the other *Devachan* [1] or ' a happy place '.

Nirvana is a final human achievement. The word is often taken to mean total extinction,

[1] Pronounced dayver-tchun. The word, contrary to common belief, has no connection with the *devas* or gods or angels. The confusion is due to faulty transliteration.

abolition of individuality, and therefore as leading to a complete void. Certain scholars, among them Professor Ernest Wood, realize that it means, as he puts it, the destruction of all *false* images of selfhood. This leaves room for the basis of all identity or *ahamkāra* in a form unrecognizable from the viewpoint of the ordinary, psychological or personal ego. It is as if Self were to be reduced to a mathematical point, having no dimensional extension in time and space, no attributes except position or Being, no sphere of influence except that of the infinite universe, and so on. It is taught that whatever one may say about the Absolute or Parabrahm must at once be qualified by adding, ' It is also not that but the opposite also '. It is evident that the same paradoxical position applies to the state (which is also not a state), of nirvana. Nothing one can say about it is unqualifiedly true, and it is easier to say what it is not than what it is.

The concept can, however, be to some extent clarified in terms of the individual human being if we think of the nirvanic base of Self as a nucleus of unique and unduplicated potentiality. It is, however, in its pristine state (using the inadequate language which is all we have) unconscious, latent, immobile, completely 'transparent' to the divine Ground so often described as Absolute Light. However faulty the latter description may be, since Absolute Light is also Absolute Darkness, known in Egypt as 'the Dark Light', it suggests an analogy which will serve. There is, in the primal stage, depicted as the innocence of Adam in the Garden of Eden, no interference with the rays of the Light. When, however, individuality begins to move out of latency it becomes in some measure opaque. The result is that under the right conditions it will cast a shadow, since the Light does not pass freely through it. This condition is if some material or quasi-material object exists onto which this shadow is projected, so that a negative image of the basic Self is formed. This image will be clear and focused if the receiving object is itself smooth and plane, distorted if it is not.

In fact the shadow is cast onto the screen of the animal mind, a more or less organized, coherent and conditioned field at the level we call psychic. The shadow [1] is the personal ego, shaped and coloured by the nature of the 'mind-stuff' in and on which it comes into being. It is not a clear and perfect reproduction of the original

[1] Not to be confused with the shadow in depth psychology.

Self thrown onto a virgin field but it is shaped by that field: which is perhaps why Krishnamurti appears to go contrary to the superficial view of selfhood, and tells us that the personal self is created by the mind and only exists so long as that mind exists. Yet without the basic Self there could be no personal ego, so it is reasonable to assume that what is meant is that the *form* of this ego depends on the mind and its disturbed nature, and can only be replaced by a picture of the true Self when that mind becomes united, smooth, and poised.

Nirvana, then, is something absolute and outside the realm of space and time. Devachan however is the 'shadow' of nirvana in the same way as the personal self is the shadow of absolute Self-identity. It is 'happy' because it is only reached as the conflicts in the individual psyche are resolved or drop into latency during the earlier phases of the after-life. As the stresses and strains caused by these conflicts lessen, so does the psyche become 'happier' until (according to tradition) there is no more strife at all, and he enters the heaven or paradise of devachan.

Nirvana is a state which is, one might say, *achieved*, while devachan is *earned*. The achievement of nirvana depends only indirectly on good deeds

and right thinking, for these are the sequel, not
the cause of the opening of inner consciousness:
one cannot be even partly enlightened and aware
and at the same time do wrong or hold false beliefs
for long. The final step is one which removes the
individual self from the realm of causality, of existence, and it enters that of a-causal Being. Devachan,
however, is a sequel to whatever is ' good ' and
' right ' (these terms have to be used carefully
and with many qualifications, and not as referring
to any absolute standards) in the character of the
individual. It still belongs to the world of causes,
and in that sense can be said to be a reward for
past acts. It stands for the working out of forces
set going by the individual within himself, just as
he set going those which have tied him down to
the purgatorial state from which he is emerging.
It is a self-created heaven, built up and around
the individual's own thoughts and desires; and it
follows that whatever he wants will be there just
as he wants it, and whatever he does not want
will be automatically not there: else it would not
be heaven. In this sense it might be called a Fool's
Paradise, using the word ' fool ' for the man who
is still tied to the world of time and form because
of his ' ignorance ' of the roots of life.

Nirvana is a condition which is above time, perhaps even above eternity as we consider it: it matters nothing to the nirvanee whether or not he re-enters the time world. He is an ' *Arhat* ', an enlightened man. The devachanee, however, is enjoying something which is still temporal and so, however long his period there in terms of earth-time, temporary.

From the point of view of our text, the difference is of prime importance. In Christian philosophy there does not appear to be any distinction between the true and the ' false ' or mayavic states of bliss, and the two seem to have become confused in a wishful notion that the good man goes to heaven and stays there permanently. The eastern view, however, is more in line with what seems logical and probable; and when we come to consider the problem of continuity, its value will appear all the more.

In conclusion let me make it clear that this summary is a very brief and simple one when compared with the elaborateness of the descriptions of the various *lokas* or psychic worlds to be found in many of the ancient writings, and in such modern ones as H. P. Blavatsky's books, or in *The Early Teachings of the Masters* or *The Mahatma Letters*.

For present purposes we need not delve further into these nor try and determine how much of the teaching refers to actual 'places' in the psychic world, how much to subjective states of inner consciousness.

11

COMMUNICATION WITH THE DEAD

IT has always been held that the dead can, at least under certain circumstances, communicate with the living. There are endless stories of haunts linked with particular individuals; people have dreams which bear the hallmark of truth; and, of course, the more credulous spiritualist accepts at face value the spoken or written material emanating from mediums. A careful analysis of this matter will be found in our own book, *This World and That*, where the psychological implications are more fully explained, but a brief recapitulation of the principles comes into the present theme.

Modern psychology knows that the mind is not homogeneous. It largely endorses the views of clairvoyants who describe the ' aura ' or psychic organism as consisting of various layers, as well as of patches of colour, more or less well defined yet differing in different places. However this may be in fact, it fits with the psychologists' view that the mind is made up of units of thought and feeling gathered together and ' constellated ', to use Jung's word, round the centre of personal I-ness, the ego. The analogy of the body, with organs controlled by the brain and the autonomic system, suggests itself, but the psyche is less rigidly formed, the units often overlap and, if they become detached, may even acquire a large amount of independences possibly becoming almost complete personalities in themselves. To what extent this tendency comes into action depends on individual temperament, the strength of the ego-centre, the degree of self-awareness and integration of the person.

The units are called ' complexes ' by the psychologist, who sees them as more or less organized systems of thought and feeling within the totality of the mind. Some are linked directly with consciousness, some are not—though there is no sharp division between the conscious and the unconscious mind—and they are often interlinked. A better word for these units, for purposes of our discussion, is that of Whately Carington,

' psychons' or psychic units. We shall use it here if only because it serves its purpose well and avoids the pitfalls of the word ' complex ' about which different schools of psychiatry have their own ideas.

The psychon, as we have said, is characterized by power to function independently of the central ego. It may even be said to have something of a centrifugal tendency which enables it to move out of control of the ego. If it does so it becomes projected out of the field of the psyche, in which case it becomes autonomous, with the characters perhaps of a very complete personality in which case it includes at least some fragment of the ego-centre; or it may be something less than complete, when it is more of a lay figure, possibly with an active but automatic routine of behaviour which it goes through when circumstances set it in motion —much as the processional figures found on medieval clocks spring into action at a given time, then subside again into latency.

To some extent every individual projects his mental contents onto the world around him, and they become attached to objects and people by desire (*kāma*). This desire may be either towards or adverse to them. Thus a favourite chair receives something of the mind of its owner, a person who has qualities the individual does not like in himself becomes an enemy (it has been truly said that there are no enemies which you yourself have not created) or a person one dislikes, and so on. The psychon corresponding to that object tends to ' gravitate ' towards it and, to use a spatial terminology, to stay with it. Another form of projection is where a ' thought-form ' acquires a life of its own. Many novelists know how a character invented by himself—that is, originating from his own inner mind—may become so much alive that it takes control of the story, leaving the author almost in the position of a Boswell recording the doings of a Dr. Johnson. Such a phenomenon undoubtedly accounts for many of the guides of mediums, not to mention the images of Masters and other great spiritual Beings among students of the occult. It should be added, in the latter case (and the principle applies as much to theosophical students as to people like monks and nuns who see visions of Christian saints or of the Christ) that genuine spiritual aspiration gives these images a certain quality which, however much it is a product of the devotee's own mind, nevertheless uplifts and is therefore ' genuine ' despite the fact that the *form* of the vision is self-generated.

The important principle in the whole matter is this ability of the mind to split itself up without of necessity causing mental disease. It is only when a breakdown of the psychic fabric occurs that serious trouble arises and the conscious field becomes invaded by things and ideas which do not normally belong there. Jung, speaking of the insane, tells us that, ' In most cases where a split-off complex manifests itself (in physical consciousness) it does so in the form of a personality, as if the complex had a consciousness of itself. Thus the voices heard by the insane are personified '. He clearly refers here only to projected contents of the patient's own mind, and not to any direct vision of the psychic world in its own right, external to this mind; though such a thing occasionally happens as a result of the breakdown of the screening mechanism between the psychic world and physical consciousness. (It may be added that this is very much rarer than many ' psychics ' aver and the visions of most insane people are simply of the contents of their own minds.)

Thus we have before us a picture of a mind which is able to divide itself, almost as primitive animals do, by fission. But whereas the amoeba or the yeast-cell reproduces itself entirely, the psychons which may bud off from the mind are not complete, and often represent only fragments of the whole personality. They can best be described as thought-forms (thought always including feeling) built by habit and related to a place, an object, a person or perhaps to an abstract situation (as in the case of the novelist's characters). They are shaped by thought, given life by feeling or, to use the psychological term, *libido*, meaning psychic energy; and they tend to attach themselves to some physical place through the force of the libido or desire related to that place.

It does not therefore in any way follow that the ghost in the churchyard in the form of a little old lady repeatedly trotting from vicarage to church is the lady herself. It is a psychon left behind when she died, and kept in being by the emotional charge connected with her devotional life. Even where, as in the case of banshees or other phenomena connected with impending events, there is a strange and uncanny precognitive quality about them, there is the same automatic sequence of events in what they do as in any purely mechanical device.

Further, apart from the very obvious wishful thinking of mediumistic communications, it is reasonable to doubt whether any intelligent ' dead ' person is likely to attend seances in person. At best, perhaps, some fragment of himself, a psychon attached to the sitter, may be present. Indeed, in *The Mahatma Letters to A. P. Sinnett*, letter 16 contains some very categorical statements that the dead cannot communicate with the living through spiritualistic seances, while the ' spooks ' which attend are said to be only ' shells ', discarded elements of the soul's totality: the word ' shell ' being in this instance equivalent to our own word ' psychon '.

If, however, a psychon-ghost contains a certain charge of psychic energy, it would be reasonable to expect this to run down after a time; and this indeed often happens, ghosts disappearing a few years or months after the death of the person to whom they relate. But this is not always so. Some ghosts seem to endure for many years or even centuries. Thus the highwayman who terrorises the person in an old inn bedroom seems capable of endless endurance. It seems as if in such cases there is no reason to think the actual highwayman, as a man, is present any more than in any of the other ghosts who repeat the same pattern mechanically. But it looks as if the psychons involved had a form of cunning by means of which they know how to keep themselves recharged and hence ' alive '. It is as if they drew into themselves the energy of the emotional reactions of their victims, and fed on the fear they evoke when they attack somebody. On the other hand, if the person they appear to, fails to respond in the usual way by being frightened or horrified, they gain nothing and, on the contrary, tend to lose their strength. Thus it may happen that after a very long interval when nobody has been to a deserted house, let us say, some visitor finds nothing abnormal there; while if, on the other hand, a contrary and positive emotion such as anger replaces the usual fear, it seems as if the psychon could be shattered and finally dispersed. The same thing would happen if a positive effort were made through exorcism or, alternatively, if pity or love replaced the usual fear reaction, so breaking what had previously been a vicious circle.

Psychons which haunt certain places are, however, often entirely harmless if not positively pleasant. There are many accounts of familiar ghosts which are seen at intervals by people in an old house, when they evoke no strong emotion of fear. Indeed, they may even seem to be kept alive by the affection felt for them, as where Grandfather seems to be still sitting in his favourite place by the fire. More or less consciously, his relations, by their warm and loving thoughts perpetuate the existence of the thought-form or psychon, as they remember him sitting there.

In general, it would seem—though there is no scientific proof of this hypothesis—as if the majority of ghosts were detached fragments of a personality, drawn back by emotional links to the places to which they were attached, and kept alive by being supplied with emotional energy, whether this be positive or negative, which harmonizes with the quality of that fragment. This goes on until something happens to break the supply or to shatter the form, when they dissolve.

This theory, however, does not account for all cases. We have the famous history of the two English teachers, Misses Moberly and Jourdain, who had strange experiences at Versailles, while visiting the Trianons. Their story is too well known to need repeating. It has been criticised for certain inconsistencies and historical errors, but if one is familiar with this type of material, these very faults reinforce the view that the ladies' accounts were genuine. For not only does psychic time lend itself to anachronisms, but, besides, the conditioning of the mind of the observer plays unconsciously into the pattern and adds a factor of error.

Here, however, the psychon theory, if it applies at all, would not be so simple as in the case of a single ghost or haunt. Many people feel nostalgic about Marie Antoinette and her times, however decadent they were in reality, and many would confirm the underlying glamour of the atmosphere in the toy farms and the pleasure palaces of Versailles. The psychons would therefore be less pieces of individual minds than an aggregate from many sources, keeping alive something of the drama of the actual history of the place. The same would apply to the ladies who woke up one morning in Dieppe thinking themselves to be in the midst of a battle, only to realize that this was the anniversary of a major raid in the second World War. Others have seen the Battle of Waterloo, with its great historical significance, being re-enacted on the field, and there are many similar accounts.

There are, also, some cases where the detached psychon theory seems weak compared with the idea that an actual human psyche is involved. Thus it was recently reported in a sober medical journal that in a particular hospital in Britain, a little old lady was sometimes seen by patients. She always seemed to perform some simple task for their comfort, such as bringing them a cup of tea or straightening their pillows. She was described in sufficient detail for nurses and doctors to identify her with somebody who had died not long before, yet she seemed so normal that patients only thought of her as one of themselves, convalescent. The outstanding feature was, however, that she was never seen except by a patient who died very soon after. The automatic psychon-ghost scarcely fits this case, and suggests that perhaps under special circumstances a person may be able to stay in sufficiently close touch with the physical world to use her benevolence in a highly practical manner—but only on those already half-way towards entering the after-death psychic realm. Moreover, she did not seem to fit into the category of the legendary earth-bound soul like the Flying Dutchman or the Wandering Jew, whose stories appear to be that they are tied in by their crimes or miseries in a state from which they cannot free themselves

The element of mystery persists.

The foregoing discussion has been purposely negative, in order to point out as forcefully as possible that communication with the dead is not the simple thing which many people believe. Far from this, there are statements in books of profound occultism which say categorically that it is extremely rare, if ever, that a real dead individual will grace a seance room. It is well to realise how a medium may pass on with entirely honest intent messages which emanate solely from the mind of his sitter, or from his own mind—which is why the majority are so vague, repetitive and platitudinous—or from some detached fragment—a ' shell ' or psychon—of the actual, living mind, of the discarnate individual.

This, if accepted, will disillusion some who, having lost the physical presence of a relative, are not willing to accept life—of which death is an aspect—as it is. They anxiously and often quite selfishly keep on worrying, ' Where is my husband now? ' or, ' I want to know that he is by me ', or ' He must surely still love me and wants to tell me so '. Even people who, in theory, accept the idea of continuing life out of the body often react to actual death emotionally and in a way which does no credit to their faith.

In any case, such a demand and such a search is the most certain way of courting frustration. For, regardless of any laws which govern these matters, the mourner is trying to force life to provide something for himself and his personal satisfaction instead of accepting experience and allowing events to take their natural course. If, however, a bereaved person, when as he should try and do, has overcome the first shock of being alone, can then achieve an attitude of acceptance of things as they are, he is likely, sooner or later, to realize that what he has lost is not his relationship with the departed. It is only its physical manifestation which has gone and, in the world of reality, the dead are as close to the living as they ever have been.

Indeed, it is a curious reversal of the truth to make so much of the physical presence of a person. For it is at the physical level, with its discrete, well defined body, that contact is least. Not only is the most intimate physical connection tenuous and ephemeral, but people who are concentrated on physical experience tend to obscure the inner, psychic experience which is shared between two who really love one another. In the psychic sphere, where we operate habitually during sleep as well as after physical death, there is no break between minds except as we ourselves create one. If we wrap ourselves into a cocoon of misery, we create a barrier which nothing can penetrate, and so turn our back on any psychic presence there is. And of course, to conclude our discussion of this theme, we must remind ourselves that spiritual man is not only united permanently with the rest of mankind, and therefore with every individual, but that he is actually one with it and with his fellows.

Any loss of contact with the dead is something created by oneself, maybe from lack of inner sensitivity; maybe from ignorance as to where and how to look for that which already exists in a less material form than when one is in the same physical room as a person; maybe from a grief based on false valuation, and frequently deeply tinged with selfishness and love of oneself rather than the free spirit of love for others.

If the bereaved can, however, reach a state of true and inner acceptance of what life—even in its negative form—has brought him, and of the pain he naturally feels; and if he stops even expecting or hoping for some sign from the beyond, he is likely to find growing in him a deep sense of closeness with his loved one. It may be nothing more, and yet it satisfies. He may even have a dream or vision which, directly or indirectly, shows him what he wants, and even, though perhaps more rarely, some physical event may take place which he connects unmistakeably with the dead person. But this can only happen when he himself has reached an attitude of mind far removed from that of those who rush from medium to medium in the vain hope of receiving comfort or reassurance.

12

THE CAUSE OF CONTINUITY

To many people the idea of reincarnation is today familiar. They may or may not accept it in its literal and simplest form, but it is no longer to the western mind one of the heathen superstitions it was once thought to be. Indeed, since Nature is always cyclical, carrying out her processes from beginning to end in a series of recurrent phases, it would be natural for human evolution to be true to the general pattern and itself to be phased and cyclic at least until the human stage is transcended: after that we cannot say what happens. It is only if we think of man as a body with a soul and/or spirit more or less vaguely attached to it that we can believe a single incarnation to be the beginning and end of the life-process in man. If he is seen as primarily something which, while it includes the physical body, is also largely non-physical, our conception of the human process is changed and sequential. So repeated descent into an animal-like body comes within the ambit of reason. Whether or not it is factually true that such descent is always into the kind of body we know on earth, whether it is on this planet, and so on, is less relevant than to understand the general principle of cyclic evolution, a period of activity followed by a state of external quiescence, much as we see it in every natural phenomenon.

Death, the period between this and rebirth, birth, and physical life are, from the standpoint of the Being Self, one process, existence. Seen from the level of the latter, however, they can be analyzed as in some measure consecutive in time, and so discussed from various points of view as if they were separate components of the totality of life. In ordinary life we sleep, wake, act and once more sleep, and at each moment a certain aspect of the totality is uppermost. It is in these terms that we can best discuss the question of the factors which may make for an enduring incarnating personality. This is quite a different thing from the endurance of the *individuality* in its pure form, that Self which is, outside of time and which as it were, dips down into time to fulfil certain evolutionary demands. In other words, we shall try and discuss whether, and how much of Adam Smith and Eve Brown is the result of past time-cycles and how much of them may return in the future.

The background however is that of the individual as spirit and hence the prime mover and originator of the whole process by which personality is created in the world of space and time. As it enters the realm of existence (ex: ' out,' stans: ' standing ': hence giving the meaning of something extruded from some inner state) it makes itself felt in the world which surrounds it and so creates for itself the ' existential state ' in which it lives. That is, the within plays upon the without, evoking a reaction from it and so creating the world in which it lives. It is axiomatic in Taoistic philosophy that in a certain sense Tao is what you see and experience around you at any given moment and that this is a world-image created and evoked by yourself. There is no place for accident in the common meaning of something fortuitous and ' untimely ' in the events which come to you, but that everything is determined by your own state of mind, completely fitting this from moment to moment. Jung speaks of this when he uses the word 'synchronicity' as implying that wherever an outer event takes place it reflects some inner movement of the soul. Thus, life is a constantly moving pattern which adjusts itself to individual need at every instant we exist.

It follows from this that personality both determines and is determined by its environment. 'I' in the personal sense do things to my surroundings, these surroundings react on me in a manner which, however much I like or dislike it, is entirely appropriate to what I myself am at that moment. If I fail to understand and accept this experience, I then react to it and so set up a further chain of reaction from the outside towards myself. This, in brief, is the law of *Karma* which, properly understood, not only explains why we remain bound to the wheel of causality and continuity in time, but also gives us the key to liberation.

Karma, hence, is no punitive or rewarding, moralistic law. It is, in modern scientific terms, a constant balancing up of the forces between ourselves and the world in which we exist. Nor is it a fixed process comparable to book-keeping, with entries of debit and credit on opposite pages. It is a dynamic, cybernetic or self-adjusting system in which there is a constant 'feed-back' due to the manner in which we accept or refuse experience from moment to moment. This takes into account the way in which we act in our acceptance or refusal. It may be that a true acceptance will cancel out some of the forces which tend in a particular direction, while refusal merely postpones or adds to the unresolved total situation of our lives. In other words, wrong understanding and valuation of events perpetuates the complex of forces around it, while true understanding resolves it. That is why in Buddhist philosophy ignorance is said to be at the root of all suffering and misery: lack of understanding, not anything like ' sin '. The man who understands cannot any longer act wrongly, and so be sinful.

In principle, therefore, one who knows is free. He can enter the next stage beyond that of existence and enter the realm of Being (which is also non-Being) called Nirvana, moksha and by other terms. But man individually and collectively has linked himself to the realm of time; and whatever the wise man has achieved in the realm of inner awareness and consciousness, he may not yet be free of the claims of the time-world. He may have dealt positively with the factors which led him wantonly or carelessly to set a house on fire, but that does not put out the flames nor make good his action at the physical, time level. The time-world has a kind of inertia, a drag which may postpone the immediate resolution of acts performed by a person. Free within, he may still have to work out the past even if he now does so without setting new karmic forces in motion, and so he has to return and see to these. In other words, man is bound down by the action of the karmic law until such time as he no longer has any backlog of this behind him. After this he is free.

The backlog of karma, then, is the cause of continuity. Karma is 'generated' by ignorance and lack of understanding. Delayed understanding, that is, when it comes *after* reactions have taken place, leaves something behind, but immediate understanding means immediate resolution of a situation. Hence the importance, not of past or future, but of the actual present moment, as the dynamic point in life.

It can serve as the place from which the individual steps off in another 'dimension', which Gustav Stromberg speaks of as 'the dimension of eternity'; or, as is most common if not practically universal, it is also the moment at which the individual moves on along the old dimension of time, as against eternity, and so continues the round of existence, perhaps gradually in a better manner than in the past, but still on the same line. The movement into eternity would lift the individual out of the realm of causality and of the unending chain of action and reaction, whereas failure to do this keeps him tied to it.

If we understand this principle, we see that, if we were able to do so, we could step off the treadmill of time at any moment. It explains the curious legend that when the Buddha first preached after His Enlightenment, the two thousand who heard Him were liberated on the spot, becoming in the technical sense, *Arhats*. They are not said to have been a specially selected band of holy men and yogis. No doubt some inner preparedness brought them to the spot at the right moment but, perhaps because of the atmosphere in which they found themselves, something opened up in them which enabled them to make the required mental change of direction and set themselves free. The same idea is also implicit in Krishnamurti's insistence that there is no need for years of plodding along the path of a set discipline. The Zen Buddhists echo the same idea, as does the Hindu tradition when it tells one that when one reaches the end of a discipline one has, as it were, to step off the top rung of the ladder and go on without it: the stepping-off being more important than the ladder ever was. The Dhyana Buddhist sect also speaks of the possibilities of the immediate moment, and that there is no need to spend aeons preparing for liberation, only to find that when it comes it could have been achieved very long since.

The reason for emphasising this is to show that, just as St. Paul tells us that we can be changed ' in an instant, in the twinkling of an eye ', if we could only find the trick of letting go, we could achieve this ' karmaless ' liberation at any instant and at any stage on the path of evolution. It does not lie at the end of a long period of religious and spiritual exercises only. In other words, the continuity of life in cycles of birth, death and rebirth, can be broken at any moment by the one who has somehow learned how to do it. One cynical student of the matter suggested, moreover, that our difficulty in reaching the point of liberation lay not in the complexity of the process involved but in its being so absurdly simple that our elaborate human minds were incapable of realising, not so much what to do, as how to stop doing the things we have been doing. It is activity, not inaction which prevents us from finding the door which is ever open for us to enter.

For most of us, however, it is clear that, through our own unwisdom, achievement lies ahead in time: we have not achieved in the past, and we are still, in the present, acting and reacting, and so generating the causes which tie us down. There is only one point when we can achieve, and that we have not yet reached, in time. What we need is to realize that this 'future' point could be brought into the present moment—if we were in the state of inward preparedness to take advantage of it.

Hence, the cause of continuity can be considered as due to our ignorance; or, which is in reality secondary to ignorance of the deeper laws of Being, attachment to irrelevant or 'unreal' values; or, in yet other terms, to the desires which are the links between ourselves and the objects and objectives of the material world. Were we to break those links or, rather, to let go of them at the inner and personal end, we should be free. The continuity of birth and death would no longer bind us, and that which we call ourselves would be lifted up and transformed into something real, eternal, and truly immortal.

13

WHAT IS REBORN?

OUR discussion so far has been based on the premise that man is a permanent individual whose identity exists on two levels. At one level it is the immortal Self, which IS, at the other it is impermanent though linked with the permanent, and lasting only as long as *existence* does. That is, the psychological ego belongs to the realm of time, and so is subject to change, and hence to ultimate dissolution and death.

This raises at once the question as to whether the people we know as Adam Smith or Eve Brown belong to the first or the second category. Did they live in the past, in Greece or Egypt, being much the same people as now, and will they go into the future in the same way? And if so, how much of them?

Here, neglecting the materialistic and so-called rationalistic attitude which sees the end of the individual when his body dies, we need to consider the school of thought which believes that individual existence lasts only as long as the body, but that it endures both in physical acts such as producing children and in works achieved, and as a contribution to the collective mind of man. It is said here that each man, being embedded in the large unit which extends long after, as it did long before, his physical incarnation, whatever he does merges back into the collectivity of the experience of mankind as a whole when he himself ceases to exist. This doctrine may at first sight seem to be in contradiction to spiritual teachings, yet it has much in common with pure Buddhism which, from the time of Gotama has always insisted that self-identity is an illusion, that ' I ' do not exist in reality and that it is only ignorance which allows me to believe I do exist and, in fact, actually creates the false idea that I do so.

It is from this assertion that the idea arises that Nirvana means absolute extinction: which in a sense is true as referring to the personal identity. But as I have already pointed out, a deeper study of the principles indicates that it is not essential *ahamkara* or selfhood so much as *false* images of self which vanish at this point. It is as if personal selfhood were a circle which serves for a time—just as the amnion and the chorion surround an embryo—but then has to be broken and discarded, leaving only a centre: a point in the cosmos. And, as mathematicians tell, a point has no size: it does not ' exist ' yet it ' is ', showing position, and hence playing a key role in any proposition.

Buddhism, moreover, puts before us a scheme which explains the mechanism by which the basic Self manifests in the realms of the psyche and the body. This is the doctrine of *skandhas*. This word, variously translated as ' bundles ' or ' heaps ' of attributes, and also as ' branches ' (from the Self) suggests that, as it were, attached to that Self emerging from the world of Being into that of existence, there are certain foci, certain nuclei, from which and to which response takes place. It is difficult to find exact description of them, and later theosophical writers have used the term ' permanent atoms ' for them, attempting to link them with the ' matter ' of the various levels of nature. In any case, they seem to act as collectors of experience of various kinds, as well as centres from which outgoing action takes place. They can be thought of as originally simple and abstract, but, in the course of evolution, gathering material round themselves and so justifying the idea of 'heaps' or 'bundles'. They are the basic axes of the personal—i.e., psycho-physical—individual. At death, it is said, they become inactive, latent. At rebirth, it is they which, interacting with their environment, produce the personality of each life.

The interaction between them, as subjective foci of force, and the environment is determined by the demands of karma. Thus the pattern of the personality, as manifested, is not of necessity the same from life to life, while the basic material remains the same—except in so far as integrated evolutionary experience transforms it and the skandhas with it. It is only at the end of the human stage of development, when the Arhat is about to enter Nirvana, that the skandhas finally dissolve, 'break apart', letting the individual Self free.

Considered from this angle, Adam Smith and Eve Brown as we know them in their personalities, are a pattern of skandhas, developed by their own past experience and shaped temporarily by the karma of their birth and early lives. But in another life, the manifest pattern may be quite other: the same assembly of skandhas being born in a different country and race, sex, and so on, and called into activity with a different enphasis and a different overall balance. The new personality would no longer be recognizable as Adam Smith and Eve Brown; yet if one were to be able to look below the surface, one would find there Eve and Adam, no longer Brown or Smith (I have purposely used archetypal names for basic human beings for the two, to indicate their time-enduringness). It is therefore Adam and Eve who are reborn, the essential and timeless Self of each being always in the background, however little they might be aware of it during their physical—and, for that matter, their psychic—life.

There does, however, come a time when human beings cease from being automatic, instinct-ridden super-animals, however intelligent they may be in mundane affairs. This is the moment described by various thinkers as the ' second birth '—a title as premature as that which dubs man today *homo sapiens* or ' wise man '. Rather are we concerned with a second conception, leading eventually to rebirth.

This second conception is that where man turns from purely material considerations and begins to think of spiritual matters, of God, of the meaning of life. This stage is often well illustrated in individual lives where a person suddenly or gradually changes from deep within himself. It is at this point that the depth psychologist finds his patients beginning to dream of archetypal images, which are in effect symbols projected from the spiritual world and given form in the mind. What is taking place is that the deep, true Self is beginning to make itself felt in the personal psyche, entering the field of the conscious mind, and bringing with it new forces, new energies and therefore new potentials for the personal man. We now have an overall change in Adam and Eve, our two human characters. The timeless, as against the merely time-enduring, is entering actively into their humanity, and this is likely to begin to give a certain consistency to their life-cycles which was not previously apparent. Whereas in the past different facets of their total personal pattern showed forth from life to life, now there is more of a sense that these facets are not separate but that they belong to a greater whole. They themselves are flat, two-dimensional, but there is at least a hint that these flat surfaces belong to the same underlying diamond and, as time goes on, the quality of the diamond tends to come increasingly to the fore.

What, then, has happened to Adam Smith and Eve Brown? We have already suggested that they have changed their surnames each time they dipped down again into incarnation. And now both Adam and Eve are changing their deeper attributes. Yet it is they who are reborn and who endure until the moment eventually arrives when they symbolically return to the nirvanic Garden from which they were expelled, which is also the mansion of the Prodigal's Father, and they once more become one with Him: but they return with the self-consciousness and awareness which is the fruit of their long pilgrimage. Adam and Eve, hence, become immortal as they die to the world of men and their little, personal self merges back into its source.

In thus outlining what suggests itself as the normal course of things between lives, I feel that a footnote is needed in view of the special conditions obtaining in the world today. Exceptional situations may call forth exceptional results, and there is no denying the peculiarity of the present century with, so far, two major wars and very complete social and political revolutions in all parts of the world.

From our point of view, this appears to have affected the quality of the people of the world in what may be a short-circuiting of the usual full cycle. This is suggested by the number of strange children in our midst. Some of course are so because of indiscipline and mismanagement or instability in their homes. But any careful observer, especially if he has worked among the problem children in clinics, realizes that some, whether they come from good and stable homes or from broken ones, carry with them a special quality which can only be described as maturity of mind and feeling. They may be far less attractive than many a more ordinary child; they may not be particularly brilliant or intelligent; and indeed they are only too often trying, however interesting, to bring up.

Their chief characteristic is the adult quality of their minds. And it suggests that perhaps, from among the millions of people, many of them in their physical prime, who were killed in our two wars, a considerable number somehow were enabled —or obliged—to return to incarnation without undergoing the gestative period of the *Bardö* or intermediate life. They come back with adult psyches which are too much of a load for infant nervous systems, thus causing physiological problems; while the child body, refusing to behave so that the grown-up mind can express itself freely, leads to psychological difficulties. I have often found that if such a child is approached, not as from the standpoint of an adult talking to a junior, but on the level, as man to man—as far as may be, when language and physical strength are still those of a child—an understanding is reached. This at least allays the protest against lack of understanding which is often the cause of bad behaviour. If parents can accept the situation, even if only as symbolic rather than as a fact as foreign to them as reincarnation, the results are sometimes quite surprising. A new relation of mutual respect replaces the old exasperation of one with another—especially if the child is, as is often the case, far more adult in mind than his parents!

Proof of this there is none: but practice makes the idea worth considering.

14

TWO PARADOXES

THE reader may have noticed that I have written of the psychic world and its content in terms which leave it in doubt whether or not it is being considered as material—i.e., made up of particles —and hence very similar to, if less dense than, the physical. Some believe it to be so, and speak of the matter of the various ' planes ' of existence as made up of atoms of varying sizes, the smaller aggregating into larger ones to make a more material or denser order of particles. Indeed one writer has calculated exactly how many of the most spiritual, and hence finest, material are required to make up one physical atom.

This purely materialistic attitude is, however, shaken by the scientists' view of matter today. This view may stand as a symbol or a glyph, but it is very far from factual, and the analogy of gas dissolved in water, the water absorbed into sand, the sand penetrating a heap of pebbles, may help to explain matter to some extent but goes no further towards the truth than any other analogy. For science today realizes that what we call matter is merely energy. There are no solid particles, though, when the energy ties itself into knots or vortices instead of radiating in open curves or lines, the vortex behaves precisely as if it were such a solid object as we know in the physical world, with inertia, mass, gravitational effects and so on. But in fact the relative behaviour of such matter in regard to free energy depends very much on what is called energy levels: the amount of energy involved, whether this be in the form of heat, motion, electrical charge, etc. Moreover, the quantum theory tells us that energy can be subdivided only up to a certain point, each 'packet' or 'particle' of energy being a *quantum* which, in the case of light is known as a *photon*. In other words, physical energy-matter cannot be broken up beyond a certain point, the photon being the smallest unit.

This point is important because it gives some substance to the notion of 'planes' as being in a certain sense discontinuous densifications of ultimate matter; for the principle suggests that each step in such densification must be of a certain minimum amount, going in steps and not a smooth curve. That is, each step represents a new energy-level and depends, not on size of atoms so much as on the amount of energy [in quanta] or "lumps" locked up in the units or atoms which make up that plane.

This scientific approach to the matter is also that of the older occult tradition, where it is said that matter came into existence through the act of primordial energy, sometimes called Fohat. Fohat plays on a virgin substratum which may correspond to the older scientific idea of an ether of space, since dethroned but tending to return as a concept in the minds of research workers, and which seems to correspond to the Hindu idea of *Akasha*, the sub-substance of all manifestation.

It is easier for most people to think in terms of the material interpretation of the universe than it is in the energetic, and it is from this that the idea of psychic bodies emerges. But the more modern and scientific attitude which sees all forms as essentially due to fields of energy or 'standing wave patterns' is more dynamic and forceful to the modern mind. It is true that forms exist: but if we consider a magnetic field, do we consider it as a ' body '? Or does it create a ' body ' for itself only when iron filings are sprinkled round it and fall into a certain shape around the actual magnetic lines of force? In other words, when we see a form, do we see, not the energetic or vital basis of that form but something gathered together from a *lower* energy-level than the actual origin of the phenomenon itself?

If we consider our own dense body, we soon learn that what makes it what it is, a living organism, exists at a higher energy-level than the body itself. It arises out of a field of energies (biologists today do not go beyond the concept of electricity, into the subtler ' vital ' levels) into which, in effect, dense matter silts and builds up that compact entity which we leave behind at death.

At the psychic level the ambiguity is still more marked. For some psychic investigators tell of an emotional body as distinct from a mental or thought-body, and even describe their appearance in somewhat different yet basically overlapping terms. It is however permissible to suggest that this is due to imperfect observation and to the fact that what they ' see ' is not the emotional energy-level itself, but the reflection of this into denser matter, or a lower energy-level (however one prefers to think of it), thus suggesting colour, an ovoid form and other common descriptions of an ' aura '. The dynamic, ever-moving and evanescent quality of the emotional aspect of man are thus materialised and given a semblance of static structure which is no more real than that the dense tissues of our body are permanent and fixed. The same of course applies to the thinking level, though thought tends to be structural, and complementary to the free-flowing energies of feeling.

The pictures which have been drawn of auras, thought-forms, etc. as also those of psychic entities, are therefore only to be taken as reflections of the reality behind them. Even if perfectly observed *as forms*, they do not represent the thing itself in its real character. These pictures often help a student towards a concept of the non-physical world, but it would be a mistake to take them as more than pragmatic, serving for a time but needing to be more deeply considered if they are not to become obstacles to real insight. The same applies to all materialistic description of the inner worlds in which man lives.

The resolution of the paradox lies in the fact that, just as the scientist uses whichever description of energy-matter best suits him for a particular purpose, so can this be done with regard to the psychic and even the spiritual realm: even this last is classed in Hindu thought as belonging to the realm of *māyā*, relative or conditioned truth, and hence of illusion, not to be taken as having absolute value. The prime condition for the student is, however, that he remembers that whatever form he employs, it is only partly factual in the light of truth.

ii.

The second paradox concerns the problem of what is subjective and what is objective in psychic and, for that matter, spiritual experience. This is a matter of consciousness, of the impact of things on the central knower in the mind. Hence it is far from being as relatively simple as the first one. It is however important in the study of discarnate life which begins, so it seems, in the world of mind itself, whatever higher reaches the individual Self may later enter.

To many people the only real world is the physical, where objects have consistency of shape,

size, duration, which appear not to depend in any
way on the existence of the man observing them.
Everything else is, if not unreal, at least, subjective.

There is a certain validity in this contention if
we think of the principle suggested in one of the
schemes of envisaging man, where he is said to live
through five principles, in a fivefold world, the
dense physical body not being one of them. This
differs from the septenary system where the physical
body at one end of the scale, and the highest or
" monadic ", are included as human principles,
part of the whole man.

For present purposes the fivefold view is most
useful and may help to clarify matters. For if
the dense physical world is thought of as one with
which the human being is in contact but into
which, as psyche, he does not actually enter, it
means that his relation to that world is different
from that to the realms which he actually inhabits.
He affects the dense world actively, and perceives
it receptively, through organs designed for that
purpose in the body. The five sensory organs
are well known, but western philosophy, unlike
the Hindu, does not speak of the organs of action
which, like those of sensation, have their roots in
the mind and grow out from there into the body.

These *karmendriyas* are given as voice, hands, feet, and excretory and genital systems.

What this amounts to in practice is that the human being normally plays into the dense physical world only *indirectly*, his body acting as a kind of two-way electrical transformer where earth-energies in one direction and psychic energies in the other, operate through *induction* and not direct quasi-electrical *conduction*.

This contact with the dense world is achieved at the state mythologically depicted by the moment when Adam and Eve, becoming self-conscious, put on their ' coats of skin ' and took on animal bodies already prepared for them and ready to be adapted to their own human ends. As Teilhard de Chardin tells us in his remarkable book *The Phenomenon of Man*, man is not an ordinary animal living only in the sphere of biological instinct, but one whose home is in the *noosphere* or psycho-spiritual realm. It is in the latter rather than the former that he evolves; and indeed, the human body, from the viewpoint of the zoologist has changed very little over millions of years. It has developed no radically new organs such as lungs as against gills, but has, physically, merely enlarged and elaborated the animal organ of mind, the brain.

One other useful thing the animal has provided, which is the skin. This delimits the physical field of the creature, all that is outside this skin being clearly separated from that which is within. To man, the ' real ' world, that of physical objects which exist in their own right apart from him, is fairly easy to distinguish; and indeed, it is not long before the small child learns to know the difference between things outside his body and those inside, though at first he confuses the two.

In the psycho-spiritual realm, however, the differentiation is for a much longer time not so clear. There is no firm psychic skin around the mind, which therefore tends to merge into the general world of the psychic ' planes '. At best there is a partial differentiation between the collective field or the psychic ' plane ' and the individual mind, and it is only in much later stages of human evolution that the ' I ' learns to detach itself from identification with this field. As Jung points out, the individual is inevitably influenced by the collective mind of the community, and in turn influences and modifies that collective by what it puts out from itself.

Assagioli (without going into irrelevant details at this point) completes this scheme by showing the personal self as the nucleus of a cell, related to another order of Self, from which it derives. So he echoes the principle that it is only as the personal ego centre becomes functionally replaced as the centre of cognition by this higher or deeper Self that true psychic objectivity is reached.

Before this end is achieved, however, we have to try and consider the state of the average man whose principal working centre rests in the personal ego, and in the field of the workaday mind: for it is he and not the liberated Self who passes in and out of the physical into the psychic world. He does this temporarily at any time he withdraws into deep thought contemplation, or sleep, more permanently when he leaves his body for good.

For him there are two aspects of the problem of subjectivity and objectivity. So long as he is in his body, if the physical world is to him the only ' real ' world, extended in time and space, that is the only one which is objective. His thoughts, his dreams, by day or night, any psychic visions he may become aware of are therefore subjective. In other words, where there is function in a certain world, this appears as subjective when viewed from a level more material or ' lower '. If we were able to separate psychic activity from spiritual awareness, to the psyche the spiritual would again seem to be subjective and not objective when seen from the angle of the spiritual self though it would be objective to the *personal* ego.

This represents one dimension of the subject-object problem. There is however another aspect which concerns the psychic man after death of the body, and his experience when he has entered what for many has previously been a realm of subjective experience only. He is now living not only in a world of collective thought and feeling, but the mechanism of his own mind is built out of the ' material ' of this world. He is, moreover, ' within himself ', in a way he was not with regard to the physical world. Between himself and the external psychic world there is no firm skin such as he had in the physical body, but only Assagioli's ' semi-permeable membrane '. The permeability, moreover, will vary in degree according to the firmness and strength of the central nucleus of self, and of the thinking power of the psyche; for whereas feeling tends to flow, to unite, whether by bonds of attraction or repulsion, thought tends to separate, to ' analyse ' in the literal sense of the word, and so strengthens the control of the individual as to what he allows to flow into and out of what he feels to be his own being. But the process is not complete and, indeed, the personal mind can never be entirely isolated from the collective else it would starve and insanity would follow; or, on the other hand, if there is no separation at all, the individual becomes a complete puppet of the collective, unable to assert himself as a person in his own right.

In principle, the same applies to this level of existence as to the physical: that which is outside the individual personal field is objective and what is inside is subjective. The great difficulty is to know which is which: a matter which every competent sensitive knows, but which the negative psychic usually fails to appreciate.

To put the problem briefly: if a person, whether in full physical life, at the point of death, or, if accounts are anything like correct, after death, perceive a person, an angel, a demon, is that person seeing actual entities or the projected contents of his own mind? The student of the occult often tends to take the first point of view; the psychologist, with probably much better reason, tends to take the other. Deeper study of occultism tends to suggest that the psychic world is indeed not devoid of a fauna and a population of its own—including ' dead ' human beings, those asleep, or unconscious from other causes, and living entities such as angels, ' elementals ', and so on. When a dead person again becomes aware after the period usually said to exist, of ' swoon ' or ' sleep '—i.e., of inturnedness, during which perhaps, the consciousness is lifted up in the way the dream about the doctor puts it, " right up to God "—what is it he perceives? For, if the principles advanced earlier really tell what happens, he walks into an environment which precisely fits his condition of mind and feeling. The personalized or formed objects he sees are all personally significant to himself at each stage of his after-death journey.

The view of so eminent a thinker as Jung is that the dead man finds himself becoming conscious in a world of which the denizens are in effect his own projected psychons. The occultist inclines to the view that he has as it were travelled into a world and a populated environment much as he might have taken a journey on earth. The student may however see that in practice there is no need to choose between the alternatives as if they were utterly incompatible. He will realize that it matters in one sense little if the ' helper ' or ' teacher ' of the dead man's soul is an independent being or whether he is a personalized aspect of the dead man himself, provided the result is that resolution and understanding of conflicts follows.

In actual fact it is probable that the dead person is both living among his own thought-forms and that external beings are in contact with him, the two being related by a kind of resonance between inner and outer conditions at any and every moment. And once again the practical aspects of the matter seem to overshadow the theoretical, and either interpretation may, as in the previous section, be used according to convenience—and with the same caution as to giving them absolute value. In Taoist Philosophy particularly, it is emphasised that the external world, at all levels, is from moment to moment a mirror image of the inward state. Hence, what we perceive at that moment, whether it be objective or subjective, tells us equally validly about ourselves: provided we understand it and accept its significance.

15

PREPARING TO DIE

BIRTH and death are inevitable and take place at a time about which we, as individuals, have little choice. Perhaps people who have reached a high degree of self-awareness and hence of freewill may be able to determine these things for themselves, but the average man is carried on the track of time without having much say in what happens to him. Here and there one meets people who tell that they seem to remember being offered before birth a choice of the kind of incarnation they were to have, relatively easy and comfortable, or else difficult and painful, when they would be liquidating karmic debts, but they are few. In actual incarnation, more control seems possible, in that some people try to escape by conscious and deliberate suicide—a futile act in reality—and sometimes unconsciously by falling ill and dying young. Suicide by illness is recognized among psychotherapists as one of the retreats from life when it seems past bearing; though it has to be allowed also that early death may represent simply the positive end of a particular karmic situation.

The normal mode of dying is of course old age and it is for this that some preparation appears possible.

First, it is necessary to realize that, contrary to the popular western view, death is an entirely natural and hence happy event. The strivings of western men to ' fight for their lives ', to prolong the survival of old and decredit bodies, perhaps in a state of virtual mindlessness, is quite against nature. It is based on the most primitive animal urge to protect itself and to avoid what will destroy the physical form, but man has carried this to absurd extremes when he uses heroic means to keep a person alive in a pain-wracked, shattered body when death would obviously be a release.

Moreover, as the quotation at the beginning of this book tells us, death (and Dr. Bro might just as well have added ' birth ') is nothing new but an event we have met before, something as often repeated over the ages as going to sleep at night. And, while one may justly be afraid of *how* one dies, the act of dying is in itself nothing but the continuation of a natural cycle. Fear however comes in when people dread the unknown. They may be afraid that there is truth in the more lurid stories of punishment, they may fear that what they call ' I ' will vanish (though why that should matter is not a question which can be logically answered). Some on the contrary, fear the unknown so much that they want to get the ordeal over quickly—which is one of the causes of suicide; while the one who feels guilty may virtually condemn himself to capital punishment in expiation of his supposed crimes.

But those who have approached death from the point of view of the life-cycle need have no qualms. And indeed it has often struck observers how, as the actual time for death approaches, even a tense, frightened person tends often to become serene and happy if only in a passive, negative way.

Jung suggests that old age, far from being a tattered remnant of a previously active life, is a time which, properly used, can become highly fruitful and profitable. If the mind is not, as he says, ' petrified ', the very fact that physical activity becomes restricted allows of deeper and more creative inner work than is possible in the turmoil of younger days. The possibility of contemplation and meditation grow as the body weakens, develops new ailments, becomes less able to move around. And, contrary to what might be expected, life itself becomes more and more interesting and rich as one sits back out of the moving stream and learns to watch and observe it. The mind discovers new aspects of familiar things, hitherto taken for granted and overlooked; retrospection carried out without nostalgia for the so-called happy days of youth (and how rarely they were truly happy one soon discovers if one is honest) becomes a study of the pattern underlying one's life; and old men's dreams may become an intuitive foreshadowing, if only in general terms, of new opportunities and fulfilments to come.

It is certainly a mistake to try and prolong youth by force. There are many old people who try and carry on their work when they are far past doing it really well. They argue that they are indispensable—and nobody is. They say there is no one who understands what is wanted as they do—and that may be true because they have been unwilling to let a junior share with them the problems of their task. They want to die 'in harness' as a matter of pride, where a realistic view would show them that they would be more useful as senior counsellors, ready to give advice when asked, allowing others to become experienced in the place they occupied. And, of course, constant activity stands in the way of gaining understanding and facing reality.

This the Hindus understood when, of old, it was laid down that after the earlier phases of being first a student, then a householder and breadwinner, it was right and proper for a person to become a *vanaprasta* or hermit, then a *sanyasi* or contemplative. Much as this principle has deteriorated and become commercialized—the 'holy man' being only too often anything but holy, and mainly concerned with getting the necessities of life out of others without doing any work—the idea is sound even today, and in the western world.

External behaviour is however only one aspect of the whole matter. For there is also inner, mental behaviour to be considered; and this is perhaps more important even than what one actually does in one's daily life.

There are two main sides to this. One is whether, in reviewing the past one is willing to

see and to admit the mistakes one has made, to
realize the place egotism has played in one's
decisions, and, seeing these faults, to see also that
the time has gone when these things were done.
Too many people tend to dwell on the past with
a sense of guilt which does no good. It merely
ties the individual down without improving what
went wrong. The positive attitude is to admit
the mistake and then pass on. The same applies
to past glories: the position achieved, the self-
importance it fostered, are real enough, but those
too belong to the past and cannot now be changed.
In other words, here is a chance of realizing the
wiles of the personal self, and if this is done with
a certain light-heartedness and with the ability
to laugh at oneself in a kindly way, it brings about
a sense of freedom and liberation. Bunyan's
Pilgrim came to a point on his journey when he
was at last able to drop his burden, and was thence-
forward able to travel all the more rapidly and
happily towards the goal. We should do the same.

Many people in their last years, months or even
weeks seem to achieve something of the kind. A
difficult, cantankerous character sweetens and
becomes serene, all that is best comes to the surface,
and death comes peacefully and happily. But

there is sometimes what seems to be an unexpected difficulty, which is that some do not seem able to break the link with their bodies, to let go of the organism they have inhabited so long.

Physiologists and psychologists have learned that what is known as the ' body image ' is a factor which exists in the mind of every person. So long as the body is intact the individual is unconscious of it. The moment something goes wrong, he knows pain or discomfort; and if the nervous system is injured, strange gaps and distortions of perception occur. The ' phantom limb ' of the amputated seems to belong to this order of habitual perception. It is as if there were a complex or psychon ' shaped ' to the body, which normally enjoys a considerable degree of autonomy and justifies those who say that the body has an ' elemental life ' of its own, primitive, crude, and unwilling to break up by death. It may be said to belong to the animal, subhuman order of life from which in fact it emanates. It is in that sense, and at certain levels, not part of the human mind at all; but man tends to think of his body as himself, to identify himself with it, whereas his true relation to it is that of the rider to his horse—a form which commonly occurs in dream symbolism.

If, however, this matter is thought of consciously and deliberately, it seems as if it could help old people both to live mentally in a more positive manner, and also, when the time draws near, to find it easier to let go of their attachment to the physical world.

The stories of the death of three different people may illustrate the matter. One was a deeply spiritual clergyman of the Church of England, learned, inwardly experienced, and thoughtful. But he had never considered his body as something apart from himself. He took three years before he achieved a much desired death, and during that time he was in physical misery.

The second is that of an old lady, by no means especially intellectual or book-studious; she was, however, thoughtful and philosophical. She said for a number of years that she intended to try and slip out of her body quickly and easily when she intuitively felt her time had come. Her relatives went out one afternoon and when they came back they realized that she had undergone a profound change. She said she did not feel very well and would go to bed. She was completely serene and talked freely to her daughter about what she knew was happening, commenting that it felt rather different from what she expected but that she was quite happy. In answer to her daughter's request that she should, if she could, come back and give some sign of her existence after she had died, she considered for a moment then said, ' Yes, if I can '. Soon after, she lapsed into unconsciousness and, a few days later, died.

There was an interesting sidelight to the period of physical unconsciousness which impressed onlookers, which was that her body seemed like a house without a tenant. The clocks as it were, went on ticking, the furnace kept it warm, but the one who lived in the house was away and, what is more, seemed less and less interested in her old home though she had not yet entirely left it. Then a curious phenomenon became noticeable. For several days the unconscious form seemed to hold its own without visible weakening, but the old lady's daughter, her one relative, became more and more exhausted. The daughter was in no way disturbed at the prospect of her mother's death and there were no repressed emotional undercurrents. It seemed, however, as if she were being sapped of vital energy. She did not realize what seemed to be occurring until her husband suggested that blood relatives were linked in a truly *sub*-conscious manner with their nearest family by the fact that they had common germ-plasm; and that it might serve as a subterranean channel for the body of one, at low ebb, to replenish itself at the expense of the other. The idea impressed the daughter, who realized that if such were the case, it was an illegitimate way for the body to keep alive. By a mental act she decided to cut that particular link, not with the mother she genuinely loved, but with the empty body. She dissociated herself from it so effectively that within a very few hours the mother's heart stopped and death had come, together with a feeling that the old lady was glad to be free at last. Evidently her somewhat experimental approach had not entirely succeeded, though it nearly had.

This matter of the underground link between people with close blood ties, or where a close link has been created through sexual intimacy (and all the more so if children have been born of the act) is one which has not been sufficiently described. But careful observation shows the impossibility of parent and child, or of near blood relatives ever becoming entirely objective to one another, no matter how much the psychological field has been cleared. The psycho-physical link remains, and can only be dealt with by an act of will when it is realized—if then.

The third instance is that of a very wise and deeply spiritual man who lay dying of a painful disease. The pain was dulled by drugs, which probably made it easy for him to separate himself from his body and to carry out his researches in a very practical manner. He was both a profound student of human nature and a keen psychical researcher, and he found himself able, as he told his wife, to 'go to places' in consciousness and to see things as he had never seen them before, and hence was having a most interesting time.

During the few days he lived on, the wife of his doctor, a close personal friend, woke in the middle of the night to see the man, as she described him, surrounded by a pillar of light and standing by her bed. He said to her the Latin phrase, '*Ab umbris ad lumina vitae*', then vanished. Later, she asked her husband what the words meant and he, translating the Latin, 'From the shadows to the lights of life', enquired why she wanted to know. On being told, he insisted that the matter be reported to the patient's wife, and she, in turn, told her husband. He was delighted and said, 'So it worked!' evidently knowing what he had tried to do. He died soon after in an atmosphere of complete peace, marred only by the fact that if the drugs wore off he was in considerable pain.

All of this suggests that one aspect of preparation for death lies in a gentle—not strained or anxious —mental act of dissociation of the individual's mind from the body. It is neither a morbid nor a dramatic process, but simply one of self-education, based on realization that, ' My body is my instrument and my friend; but it is not myself. Its life, while it overlaps onto mine, is not intrinsically mine, nor has it the same aims and goals as mine '. Such a thought, left in the background of one's mind and occasionally brought to the fore may be the best way of avoiding the prolongation of physical life beyond its healthy term. Moreover, while it has pragmatic application, it is based on the fundamental truth that man is not his body but something else, which uses the body only as its temporary and temporal habitation.

In principle, of course, the best way of preparing to die is where no preparation is needed. This involves living in such a way that the idea of death is always with us, together with that of life. This is no morbid *memento mori* with its common menacing implication, but it arises when one's philosophy is such that it includes both life and death as equal and complementary, neither existing in the larger pattern of Life without the other, any more than do light and shade.

The cycle of birth-growth-decay-death is only consecutive from the material angle, where between phases there may be an ordeal to undergo. From a deeper point of view they are a whole which, known, understood and accepted without cavil or reservation from instant to instant, banishes fear. And when fear disappears, serenity and freedom ensue.

16

It is clear from the foregoing chapters that the question of what happens after bodily death is not open to the simple, cut-and-dried answers which are sometimes given. There is first the need to understand the basic difference between survival and immortality, seeing the one as being *in* time, the other in a state *transcending* time as we know it. This couples immediately with the second problem of what in the human being is immortal; and from this follows a third question, what is reborn, if anything, of the person we know in incarnation, and in what form. This in turn leads on to a consideration or whether reincarnation of some sort, is a process which endures as long as time endures, or whether the individual, as Self, can free himself from its compulsion, and how.

Then we come to the matter of communication between the dead and the living; and here we have to study the nature of relationship between people in the real sense of that word, and to distinguish it from the entanglement of identification at an emotional and personal level. It seems certain that true relationships are never broken, since they rest against a spiritual and timeless background, but that personality links, based on emotional-instinctive interchanges fade as the individual first loses his physical body then, as seems to be indicated, retires more and more from external psychic involvements.

Not only, moreover, does objective thought heavily discount the validity of the common spiritualistic claims about direct personal communication, but such documents as *The Mahatma Letters* are supported by the findings of modern depth psychology and the theory of complexes or psychons, as detached units of a person's mind. In other words, they show that the communicator in a seance, is, at best, only a fragment of the dead person's whole psyche, and often not even that. The same principle helps to explain the nature of ghosts and haunts.

These are some of the main matters discussed, together with a somewhat cursory study of the deeper aspects of the factors which tie the individual to the time-track, and so to rebirth. But there is a vast context to the whole matter which has no place in this small volume. It is that of the very nature of man and of his place in the universal Whole, and even in this small corner of that Whole. In other words, starting from the purely personal and minute standpoint of being puzzled when death—or, for that matter, birth—confronts us, we can reach out from that into a study of the whole of the major problems of the universe.

These problems can be approached from many angles, through the intellect, the feelings, the arts, the sciences, the abstractions of metaphysics. One of the most coherent, and one which carries one as far as reason will go, is what is generally called Theosophy, that is, the system written down in the first instance by H. P. Blavatsky, though how much she was author and how much amanuensis in the books under her name remains a matter of debate. It is, in any case, not Theosophy—God-Wisdom—that is in her books so much as a theosophical philosophy. Wisdom cannot, as it is said in the Book of Job, be found except in the direct presence of God: and it is then that an individual becomes, in the accepted and original sense of the word, a theosophist.

The Blavatskian system is not only self-consistent, it is also consistent with the perennial philosophy of mankind. Moreover, it is not dogmatic but suggestive, in that it enters both the field of our daily experience, of history and science, but it leads out beyond into realms which the mind cannot encompass but where intuition may follow. It also contains the constant challenge, both explicit and implicit, to self-discovery. It attacks much of the superstition which passes for religion or science, while at the same time, it sheds new light and meaning on many old beliefs.

Its consistency has the danger of lending itself to dogmatism and therefore to a mental prison so that the student may find himself just as much walled in as ever. But, as with every system of myth—i.e., of symbolic presentation of Truth—if properly used and applied, and allowed to act within the mind without the attempt to formulate its ' facts ' too closely, it leads out into the light of day. It is for this reason that the study of modern theosophical works has been—to me at least— more fruitful than other systems. It bridges the obscurity of symbol and myth and the realm of ordinary thought, and so acts as a signpost to the road each one must travel for himself.

It is moreover reassuring to find how depth psychology, mythology and comparative religion, as well as scientific parapsychology, help to add new perspectives to theosophical philosophy and to build up a picture in depth. Their positive findings and their hypotheses all point towards the same goal. The sciences destroy much credulity and wishful thinking but, now that they have ceased to be dogmatic and certain, but think in terms of indeterminacy, probability, ' randomness ' (a word which merely means order not deliberately sought or produced), coincide very well with what is needed by the true seeker. For truth can never be confined in any system, it always eludes its would-be captor and leaves him with at least partly empty hands. Modern thought, however, does not deny the transcendental: it merely says, ' This is outside the field of science ', and acknowledges that there is more besides what science comprehends. In this it leaves room for much that a few decades ago was outcast.

Hence the idea of man surviving the death of the body and, more, being at a deeper level still, immortal is no longer to be taken as ridiculous superstition.   Scientific proof of this there is none: and indeed there probably never will be. We shall have to discover the truth for ourselves, by our personal efforts.   No outer teaching can take the place of this.   And when we truly know, it is probable that the time will not be far off when we shall find ourselves free of the wheel of rebirth.

EPILOGUE

In what I have written there are many flaws and loose ends. Sometimes the loose ends have been deliberately left so. We have, for instance, not gone into the nature of time, though we have touched on the manner we experience it; yet the relevance of the true nature of space and time is clear. For when we speak of a psychic movement as ' gradual ', or of things occurring ' after a time ', what do we mean? We should be able to say to what scale of time we refer, and of how it relates to clock time. When we are told that a person spends so many years between incarnations, assuming that the figures are in any sense real, to what year does one refer? For there are terrestrial years, solar years and others, all differing in duration: which, if any, is the ' real ' year? Moreover, the introspective person discovers how psychic events at times take place ' with the speed of thought ' which, as far as the clock is concerned, means, to all intents and purposes, instantaneously. Why then should an individual not go through purgatory and all other stages ' in a moment, in the twinkling of an eye '? He would then be ready for rebirth almost at once, and even the few weeks spoken of in the Tibetan *Book of the Dead* would be superfluous. There is comfort in remembering always that in occultism supposed facts are often a blind for truth. They should not necessarily be taken at face value but as coded messages which have to be deciphered to be understood. In this they are like the riddles of the Delphic Oracle, which never gave a direct answer to a question, or the Zen Master who replies by a *koan*.

There is, moreover, a provocative idea which is worth thinking about. For it seems that if one were focused at a certain level of consciousness, one would see birth, life and death in quite a new perspective, detached from the sequence of time. We usually think of successive lives in terms of the time-conditioned mind, following one another along the track of history. But in this other-dimensional awareness, the individual would be living all his lives and the periods between simultaneously. This is suggested when we hear of the moment of vision at the time of death when the whole of the individual comes into view at once: his remotest past as well, we are told in ancient writings, as his most distant future, and all that, in time, lies between. In this state it would seem that the intrinsic differences between lives, and between life and death, would not be the historic period in which they were physically lived, but the essential quality of that life: whether as a busy extravert or a contemplative monk; in the field of administration and rulership or that of teaching; as a manual worker without much outer education and only possessed of the profound wisdom of the countryman, or as a highly trained professional; with the feminine Eve aspect outermost and reflected in the sex of the body, or as the active, masculine Adam; and so on. The totality of these would indicate the pattern, the individual uniqueness, of the Man himself, and both that which was already actualized and that which remained to be fulfilled. Such an experience would not be a looking back or forward, but a real *being there at the time itself*, so that one would be at the same time the Roman senator and the negro slave, the saint and the sinner, the mother of a large family and the five-star general.

But the very idea of the timeless is open to challenge, of Being as against existence equally so. How do we know the difference? For the absence

of time is in reality merely the absence of something
we know in a certain form and from which we derive
the idea of eternal Being as against existential
life. It must be accepted that perhaps from the
viewpoint of a greater Mind the eternal is only a
passing moment on another scale or another
dimension of Absolute Time. The mind reels
before the possibilities, when one thinks that what
is to us the Absolute may be only the relative for
some other kind of being, ' Panta rhei ' says
Heracleitus, everything is in flux; and, though he
anticipated modern science by some two thousand
years and more, he might equally have said it
about the human mind when it once disentangles
itself from the rigidities demanded by instinctual
trends. The philosopher dare not speak of any
Absolute without realizing that what is to him an
Absolute is likely to be also relative in another
frame of reference, and there he has to remain: a
state of mind which causes what has been called
divine discontent because there is always the
possibility of there being more and yet more to
investigate: which is in reality the greatest joy a
man can find.

When it comes to the question of life and death,
it is only our psychic myopia which makes us

want to break Life up into categories and exact data. One who sees clearly would no longer be blinded and bound by maya, but he would see how maya itself had brought him to the further bounds of its own realm, and illumination would be at hand. At the same time he would realize the value and necessity of ' illusion ' as a means of bringing him to this point: and hence, how maya itself is an aspect of nirvanic Reality.

To him, doubtless, birth and death would appear as simultaneous and complementary processes in Life as a whole, both constantly present in every instant of time. True, to the consciousness of incarnate man there are climacterics when one or other is most prominent, as at the birth and death of a body. But, as has often been said, we begin to die the moment we are born, yet birth continues even into and after the death of the body.

Life and death are indeed māyā-filled dreams from which we may eventually expect to awake. They are like the visions of travellers in the desert who see ahead sheets of water, hills and cities; yet when they reach the place where they seemed to be there is only sand and rock, the same as further down the road. So if a man feels himself to be in life and coming towards death, life is still with him when he reaches the apparent portal; while if life seems remote, and death is one's companion, he is still by our side as we move towards the illusory goal. The wise man is he who knows this and is happy with it.

Thus, in conclusion, having reached the last page of this essay, let us round out the paradox and, looking back at the title page through the shimmer of words and ideas, let us re-read it through that shimmer and see it, equally validly as THE MIRAGE OF LIFE AND DEATH.

OTHER QUEST BOOK TITLES

For full list of Quest Book titles write to:

Quest Books, P.O. Box 270, Wheaton, Ill. 60187